RECASTING INDIA

RECASTING INDIA

HOW ENTREPRENEURSHIP IS REVOLUTIONIZING THE WORLD'S LARGEST DEMOCRACY

HINDOL SENGUPTA

RECASTING INDIA
Copyright © Hindol Sengupta, 2014.

All rights reserved.

First published in 2014 by
PALGRAVE MACMILLAN®TRADE
in the United States—a division of St. Martin's Press LLC,
175 Fifth Avenue, New York, NY 10010.

Where this book is distributed in the UK, Europe and the rest of the world,
this is by Palgrave Macmillan, a division of Macmillan Publishers Limited,
registered in England, company number 785998, of Houndmills,
Basingstoke, Hampshire RG21 6XS.

Palgrave® and Macmillan® are registered trademarks in the United States,
the United Kingdom, Europe and other countries.

ISBN: 978–1–137–27961–3

Library of Congress Cataloging-in-Publication Data

Sengupta, Hindol.
    Recasting India : how entrepreneurship is revolutionizing the world's
    largest democracy / Hindol Sengupta.
        pages cm
    ISBN 978–1–137–27961–3 (hardback)
      1. Entrepreneurship—India. 2. Small business—India. 3. Business
    enterprises—Social aspects—India. 4. India—Economic conditions—
    21st century. 5. India—Social conditions—21st century. I. Title.

HB615.S417 2014
338′.040954—dc23   2014015229

A catalogue record of the book is available from the British Library.

Design by Newgen Knowledge Works (P) Ltd., Chennai, India.

First edition: November 2014

10 9 8 7 6 5 4 3 2 1

Printed in the United States of America.

CONTENTS

To my parents, who always said, "We middle class people must always stand by the poor and take their side—and not the side of the rich."

INTRODUCTION

In the months before starting this book, I was writing and talking about the concept that I called Per Capita Hope.

In my short lifetime, it seemed as if the world's largest democracy would alter beyond recognition and finally take that lumbering leap into modernity promised when its first prime minister, Jawaharlal Nehru, spoke of its "tryst with destiny" in his midnight speech at independence in 1947.

While economists and politicians were content to debate infinitely the rise of gross domestic product (GDP) that, since India's economic liberalization began in 1991, has pulled the nation out of everlasting penury, it seemed to me that this narrow focus on GDP hid a more powerful phenomenon: the newfound freedom from anxiety and a constant sense of being held back, the paranoia of failure and the humiliation of class that millions of Indians have been freed from. No longer was success the exclusive privilege of the wealthy or the pedigreed, I argued. Liberalization had had an equalizing, democratizing role; it had allowed all of us to dream and then try to become. It had given us Per Capita Hope.

Then I had a breakfast-table conversation with my parents.

The occasion was that, at the sprightly age of 32, I had told my parents that it might be difficult for me to continue to stay with them since, you know, I might sort of move out and, you know, live with someone. Get married or something.

"Unlike your mother," said my father, carefully lowering his newspaper so that it didn't get wet on the table, as if he were saving it to read again tomorrow, "I see things practically, not emotionally. The point is—is it practical economically to run two households?

To this, my mother snapped, "Who is the girl and why does she not want you to live with us?"

I was not sure about marriage, nor was I dating anyone, but it seemed like a good time to give it some thought. The concept of marriage stressed me out, but I realized that was probably because I lived in the city of seven-day weddings that yawned on like a happy, drunken blitzkrieg until they collapsed into hangover hell.

I knew that my mother, with whom I had spent years arguing about why I needed privacy and why I wanted to lock my room, would have lots to say about this getting married and living away from home thing, but I had hoped that my father, an uncommonly peaceable man, would be, well, peaceable.

But here he was taking potshots. Like many poor government employees, my father had never had the money to get private health insurance for himself and my mother. By the time the fruits of my English-language education kicked in and I made some money as a television reporter, they were too old to qualify at most insurance companies. I had been lackadaisical about this, thinking my steadily increasing income would easily cover any health emergencies we might have.

My father, now in his mid-60s, was a more prudent man. He had recently done his calculations—even as he searched for a lawyer to make a will—and realized that his best bet was the railway medical card.

This was a card given to railway employees, for them and their spouses, that was valid for life in any of the 125 railway hospitals across India. "And if the doctors there refer us to any private hospital, the card covers treatment there too—all for free," he told me happily. "You have nothing to worry about." All these years, he had never bothered to get a hospital card partly because of that odd belief the lifelong fit have in their ability to be eternally healthy, and because conditions in government hospitals vary wildly in India and the quality of care can often be a case of luck more than anything else.

What he was not saying, but what I knew, was that my father dreaded becoming a "burden" to his only child. He had seen how disease can wipe out livelihood. Both his parents had died of cancer, draining his life savings.

In the peak of his elderly life, having refused to retire after retirement, my father continued working at least ten hours a day as a civil engineer with the Delhi Metro Rail (the city's subway system) and was pleased that he had already made provisions to ensure that I would barely have to pay anything if he or my mother ever fell ill.

But the process had left him skeptical.

"What per capita hope? Look at the prices! The builders cheat you, the private doctors cheat you, and the politicians are looting the country!" he said.

I tried to explain that it wasn't all bad, but he wouldn't listen. "I have been to various hospitals in Delhi and the ones that cheat you the least are government hospitals, and the best is AIIMS [All India Institute of Medical Sciences]. Instead of building more AIIMS, we are hell-bent on building hospitals that are like five-star hotels! Who can afford these?" he argued.

"And I counted—they must have paved the same pavement outside Khan Market at least three times before the Commonwealth Games [in 2010]. They think we are *gaadhas*! Donkeys! No one understands anything. The crooks!"

Ridden with theft that finally sent the politician in charge of the games to prison, the official budget of the Commonwealth Games[1] hosted by India in its capital, New Delhi, in 2010 was $1.9 billion—up from the $270 million estimated when the country won the bid in 2003. The politician is now out on bail.

"This is not per capita hope," said my father. "This is per capita joke!"

I had never thought that my parents would be this worried about my going to live away from them when I was in my 30s with a career thankfully going smoothly. Certainly in 2005 when I left for Bombay's TV studios, they seemed almost relieved, though tearful.

What had changed? What made them so unsure, jittery even, this time?

I've noticed, in the last year or so, that a generation of Indians who seemed so confident only a few years ago—people like me, people I met, people who earned more, less, or the same—seemed less certain about the future.

Some of it was, of course, the economy; those hairline cracks first noticed amid the tail-wagging whoops of 2007 and early 2008 had become gaping, gangrenous holes. After 20 years of ostensible reforms, we had pulled out millions of people from extreme poverty—138 million made just enough extra money to push them above extreme hunger between 2004 and 2012. But that achievement has been dwarfed, especially in the last five years, by our staggering income inequality.[2] Data from the National Sample Survey Organisation shows that between 2000 and 2012, the gap between spending and consumption by the richest and the poorest Indians had grown starkly. In 2000, the richest urban Indian was spending around 12 times as much as the poorest—this became 15 times by 2012. In villages, the difference grew from 7 times in 2000 to 9 times by 2012.

One day, faced with a full front-page ad for the iPhone 5 in my morning newspaper, I calculated that the average cost of an iPhone 5 in India would feed 1,654 people in the villages and 1,351 people in the cities.

(The average price of iPhone 5 is Rs 45,000.* India's latest poverty line, according to the government committee headed by the economist Suresh Tendulkar in 2011, is at Rs 33.3 per day in urban areas and Rs 27.2 in rural areas; people who earn less than this are considered the poorest in the country and in dire need of government help. So, 45,000 / 33.3 = 1,351.35; and 45,000 / 27.2 = 1,654.41.)

In the first quarter of 2013, Apple scored a 400 percent rise in sales in India.

It wasn't that the poorest Indians were not slowly making more money, but that the difference between rich and poor was growing much, much faster.

It's what I call the Antilia Syndrome. Antilia is a 27-floor home in Bombay built for, some estimates suggest, $1 billion, making it the costliest home in the world. There has been a debate about whether the purchase of the land it stands on—once owned by a charity that had orphanages for Muslim children—was kosher. But that debate died down after some initial flurry.

Mukesh Ambani, India's richest man and the owner of Reliance Industries, which has interests in everything from petroleum refining to large retail shops, should technically be free to build

---

*At the time of writing, $1 is equal to approximately Rs 59. The terms "lakh" and "crore" are Indian units of measurement. A lakh is 100,000 and a crore is 10 million. So Rs 1,000 = $17; Rs 5 lakhs = $8,500; Rs 1,000 crores = $168 million; Rs 2 lakh crore = $33 billion. All conversations are approximate.

any home he likes as long as he pays market value for the land and the construction. After all, it is his money.

Standing before it, though, is surreally disempowering. I am not against capitalism. Capitalism, like America for Amerigo Bonasera in *The Godfather*, has been good to me. Capitalism made my fortune, or at least let me dream of one. If it had not been for capitalism, I would not have become an author in the English language in India, for everyone knows there was a time when you could only get published if your grandfather played golf with someone, or your father played tennis with someone else.

Capitalism had kicked down the exclusive clubs of India. But standing in front of Antilia one summer day, I could see why the writer Arundhati Roy[3] wondered whether it was a "temple to the new India or the warehouse of its ghosts."

Antilia reminded us—the very poor, the slightly less so, and even those of us in the middle class—of the difference that we so wanted to forget: that unbridgeable chasm we thought we had left behind in the new India. It reminded us how far we have *not* come; that when and where it counts, there are always the rulers and the ruled. Perhaps it was pertinent that Ambani, whose father rose from working as a petrol station attendant to shatter the hierarchies of the Bombay Club of mercantile families, would choose to build a home like this. After all, his father had built a 14-story home called Sea Wind, so he probably felt the need to demonstrate his own superiority.

But unlike Roy, I did not hold that against Ambani; I was simply saddened and frightened by the reappearance in my memory of what I thought I had forgotten.

What is a nation, or indeed, a people, but a group who share a collective memory?

In his book *The Nation as a Local Metaphor: Württemberg, Imperial Germany, and National Memory, 1871–1918*,[4]

Professor Alon Confino talks about looking at German nation-hood through the perspective of collective memory, "as a prod-uct of collective negotiation and exchange between the many memories that existed in the nation." It is an approach, he says, that "explores nationhood through the metaphor of whole and parts, taking cognizance of German identity and Ger-man society as a global entity where peculiar component parts interacted."

My collective memory of India had undergone a change, a "gush-up" in Roy's words, of Per Capita Hope. But Antilia pushed it right back down. That was the problem with Antilia. Not that it was said to have a domestic staff of 600 people, not that there were said to be three helicopter landing spots on it, not that some whispered it had cost perhaps not one but two billion dollars—the problem with Antilia was that it made most of us feel static, no matter how far we had actually climbed.

And the last two decades had been all about climbing up—the sort of dramatic burst of social mobility that changes the course of a nation. We had begun to believe in an India where you might not go to the Doon School or St. Stephen's College or Oxford or Cambridge but could still do something and be someone that everyone loved and looked up to. It was a heady time that let people fantasize about escaping their pasts.

Antilia would not let us forget or escape.

When the Commonwealth Games came in 2010 and a power-ful politician showed us yet again that he could steal anything he liked at will, circumvent any law with no consequences, and laugh in our faces, it brought that ancient feeling of helplessness right back. All those years when we could do nothing, change nothing.

When the comptroller and auditor general of India announced that illicitly regulated auctions for the 2G mobile telephony spectrum had cost the exchequer Rs 1.76 lakh crores (around $39 billion at 2011 exchange rates), it was not the enormity of the sum that stupefied us, but the audacity of our rulers who, two decades after reforms, didn't bat an eye.[5]

Our anxiety was exaggerated because somewhere in the flight of our hope, we had also left our old support structures behind; now when we fell, we fell uncushioned. This, I realized, was at the root of my parents' anxiety.

My parents had been convinced that they were going to return to Calcutta, where I grew up and where we still have a home, once I was settled. But as Bengal and Calcutta grew more and more violent—first with the warring Trinamool Congress Party and the Communist Party of India (Marxist) or CPI(M), and then with the escalation of bloodshed and hooliganism after Trinamool swept to power in 2011—they gave up hope of ever returning.

As they grew older, my parents began to worry about the onset of helplessness and dependence. They had no real friends in Delhi; their extended family was all in Calcutta, as were old friends and neighbors. We were not alone in this. We were part of the C5 segment, what Indicus Analytics describes as the "eighth largest among 33 urban consumer segments, with nearly 250,000 households of around three to four members."[6]

We were what was called twice removed—immigrant and nuclear. "Nuclear families" is a curious phrase used for families consisting of only a couple and their children, in which the grandparents and/or other relatives do not live with the family. Such households in India have swelled as the traditional joint family system has crumbled. Indicus calculated that 88 percent of such households have only three or four members and no "senior members" like a grandparent in the home. Just 11 percent have more than two children—something my parents never forgot, since I am their only child. They worried about slipping and falling when I was out, about crippling disease with no one else nearby to help.

My vision of a world with a tremblingly exciting rise per capita seemed to be dying out, crashing like the rupee in tailspin. In their book *An Uncertain Glory*, the economists Amartya Sen and Jean Drèze described the income inequalities in modern-day economically growing India as creating islands of California in a sea of sub-Saharan Africa.[7] Boats that had been set afloat with much difficulty after liberalization seemed to be under the threat of sinking with a slowing economy and rising income disparity.

The cracks that we thought were getting filled seemed larger than ever. Fifty percent of Indians still defecated in the open, while newspaper headlines focused on government efforts to build a low-cost tablet called Aakash that seemed endlessly mired in controversy and ultimately found few takers.

In 2013, the Association of Democratic Reforms (ADR) said 18 percent of parliamentary and assembly candidates had had criminal cases filed against them, and 8 percent had been accused of serious crimes like rape or murder. People who were under criminal indictment and were re-contesting elections increased their wealth. More than 75 percent of them raised their assets by an average of Rs 2.34 crores, from Rs 1.74 crores to Rs 4.08 crores.

Just when the Indian capital seemed to be slowly becoming more civilized, a gang rape and murder, in which iron rods were driven into the vagina of the victim and used to tear her intestines, revealed that rapes had gone up by more than 800 percent in 40 years.

So I set out to discover this anxious India, this India the world saw when millions protested against corruption with the septuagenarian social reformer Anna Hazare, and thousands more fought pitched battles with police after that gruesome gang rape in Delhi in December 2012.

I found islands, yes, but they didn't always reek of Californication. I found pockets of incredible enterprise and dexterity that very few people ever talk about. This is a book about the extraordinary enterprise of ordinary people. People just like you and me, as annoyed, as excited, as helpless—and about how they are tackling the myriad contradictions of an aspiring country—a fascinating spectrum of journeys. These are their stories.

There are two kinds of democracies—measured democracy and experienced democracy. India is a measured democracy, which means that once every five years we can measure the number of votes cast, the vote swings and all that paraphernalia. The other is a democracy that you can feel every day, in which you feel that your elected representative actually speaks for you.

The original title of this book was *The Mango People*. It comes from an irritated statement posted on Facebook by Robert Vadra, the son-in-law of Sonia Gandhi, the president of the Congress Party, India's longest-ruling political party, and present head of the Nehru-Gandhi family, the first family of Indian politics.

In 2012, his assets and business interests were part of an exposé ostensibly showing questionable ties between Vadra and a real estate giant. The source was the Aam Aadmi Party, a reform party launched in the wake of Anna Hazare's anticorruption campaign. The revelations made headlines, but nothing really came of it because once again nothing could be proved. But Vadra was driven to the edge by the flurry of headlines and posted the line "Mango people in a banana republic" on his Facebook wall. This he later deleted, along with the Facebook account.

The phrase "mango people" literally translates to *aam aadmi* in Hindi, since the word *aam* means both "common" and "mango" (and *aadmi* means "man"). This book is for the common men and women of India. They haven't yet had their Arab Spring, or their Indian Summer for that matter, so instead, they're channeling their frustrations, fears, anxieties and dreams into entrepreneurial fervor. This is their very different tale of independence, the freedom they are only now beginning to feel free enough to even comprehend.

This book was later called *Recasting India* because that is what is happening. India is being recast, remolded and redefined. I started writing this book because I felt that a powerful moment of change in India was upon us—and it was being missed or misunderstood by much of big business and big politics, and indeed much of big media—but the people, the workers, the entrepreneurs understood it only too well. They could feel the throb and thrust of that change. They could see it play out every day, in every nook and corner. And they were contributing to that change. Their collective enterprise—in building, thinking, creating, sharing, protesting and pushing—is changing one of the oldest civilizations in the world. Even if some of that change comes with much cursing and snarling.

But what are they pushing against? They are fighting against the idea that India is, in essence, a socialist country in which the state is the key; this is a tale of India trying to rediscover, and retell, its history of astonishing enterprise. At a time when public thought in the West is increasingly telling of the demise of capitalism, when books are being written about why capitalism does not work, India is brimming with the aspiration of a billion entrepreneurial minds, what former prime minister Manmohan Singh once referred to as the "animal spirits" of the economy. In this, the Indian story is exactly the opposite of what is happening in the West, which despairs that the excesses of capitalism can never be controlled and that the destructive power of inequality is the Achilles heel of capitalism.

India has the opposite despair. When an Indian sees Antilia, he despairs not just because of inequality (though that's the story Roy and others like her prefer to focus on), but even more because of the lack of opportunity for him to build his own tower of success. Not per se a tall, tall building, you understand, but a chance to climb high and fast. This is the power of the aspiration and enterprise of millions of Indians that is not understood by most tellers of Indian tales. This is because their prism of analysis is Marxist theorizing—many of them were indoctrinated in the most left-leaning universities of America and England—and see in India's poverty only despair, not the yearning for one chance, one opportunity to break free. They believe that the state must play a welfare role—and indeed there is nothing wrong with that per se—but they fail to appreciate the role the state must play to enable enterprise: not just provide fish for the people to eat but also teach them to accurately cast the line for the biggest catch.

What does not help in this is that parts of history have been wiped out of everyday conversation.

CHAPTER 1

THE BUSINESSMAN CALLED TAGORE

When the name Tagore is mentioned, does anyone ever think entrepreneur? Not many do. The easiest association of that name is with Rabindranath Tagore, the first Indian Nobel laureate and the first non-European to win the Nobel Prize in Literature, in 1913.

Rabindranath Tagore was, like me, a Bengali. The Bengalis are known as the intellectuals and at the same time the effete of India. Both allegations are only partially true. It is true that the renaissance came first to Bengal, whose capital, Calcutta, was between 1772 and 1911 the second most important city of the Raj as India was becoming the jewel in the imperial crown. It is also true that even 30 years ago, Bengal was the cultural capital of India, producing, among others, the first Indian director to win an Oscar when Satyajit Ray, who lived and worked only in Bengal, accepted his for lifetime achievement in cinema from his deathbed in a hospital in southern Calcutta in 1992.

Today, Bengal is better known for having one of the worst rates of crimes against women in India and for elections in its villages in which scores are murdered in gun and knife battles between local political parties. Also, while generations of Bengalis have worked little to change their reputation as timid but egotistical argumentative sloths, the first and only organized army against the British Raj was raised by a Bengali intellectual, Subhash Chandra Bose. Some of the first intrepid bomb attacks on the colonial masters were the work of a Bengali, Khudiram Bose, who was hanged for murder having barely reached his eighteenth birthday. So much for being effete.

The Bengali is also said to be best fit for pontificating clerk-dom, having little or no enterprise.

But long before Rabindranath earned the epithet "Gurudev" or the "Great Master" for his innumerable works of poetry, prose and drama of rare elegance, in fact, around three decades before his birth, another Tagore was already making history.

Dwarkanath Tagore was the grandfather of Rabindranath, a man so wealthy that he earned the epithet "Prince" though, strictly speaking, in an India full of kingdoms and pedigreed loy-alty, he was merely a rich landowner. But unlike so many other landlords, who were at best profligate wastrels content with the serfdom of their poor farmer tenants and groveling servitude to the British masters, Tagore went into business.

His interests spanned coal and tea and jute, sugar refining, newspapers and shipping. In 1829, he was the first Indian to become the director of a bank. In 1834, he and his partners started the first Anglo-Indian (Indian and British) trading agency, Carr, Tagore and Company. He was a man who dreamed of bringing England's industrial revolution to the Hooghly shoreline.

In his 1976 book *Partner in Empire: Dwarkanath Tagore and the Age of Enterprise in Eastern India*, historian Blair Bernard Kling says that Tagore's dream was to take his state of Bengal, perhaps even all of India, from the mercantile to the industrial age, and put the steam engine to commercial use in the country. "Tagore organised the first coal mining company and the first steam-tug and river steamboat companies, and was among his country's pioneer railways promoters," Kling writes.[1]

As a child, I heard stories of the great wealth of Prince Dwar-kanath Tagore. Some of these were especially incredible because I am a child of Communist Bengal. By the time I was ten, the east-ern Indian state had already seen more than a decade of elected

Communist governments. From that world of load-shedding—as we called power cuts—for many hours each day, one story has remained. Invited to a musical soiree, a *jalsa* full of princes in their jewels in honor of the Queen of England herself, Dwarkanath chose to wear merely the finest white cotton with not an ornament in sight. But on his feet, each of the curling *nagra* shoes had a solitary diamond, as large as a marble, attached to the front lobe. He knew that he would have to leave his shoes outside the hall, as was the custom, and he did so, leaving the diamonds with utter nonchalance when he entered.

But in the Bengal I knew, such unostentatious elegance was already dying out, and the city was being slowly eaten from within by political thuggery so bitter and omnipotent that generations of Bengalis dreamed of escaping, as if from Cuba or North Korea. The Bengalis had long given up on enterprise, leaving most businesses to be taken over by the Marwaris from the northern desert state of Rajasthan and the Gujaratis from the west. The Bengalis had embraced glorified clerkdom like a badge and covered sloth with a sneer of intellectual pretension that has, even today, kept the state and its people primitive, in denial and clinging to the iconography of Rabindranath, the soulful poet-philosopher, but willfully forgetting Dwarkanath.

But Dwarkanath was far from being a soulless capitalist. With Raja Rammohun Roy, he was the founder of the Brahmo Samaj, the new community of breakaway Hindus fighting against the worst Hindu superstitions and rituals and turning the faith toward its core Vedantic monotheistic roots. One of the biggest battles Rammohun fought, with the vociferous support of Dwarkanath, was against sati, the horrifying ritual of women committing suicide by burning themselves on the pyres of their dead husbands.

Both Rammohun and Dwarkanath were Anglophiles. At a time when the renaissance was sweeping into Bengal, who can blame them for looking to the West for modern ideas far from the caste- and superstition-ridden, and often illiterate, environment at home?

As a result of their persistent and vocal campaigning and in the face of virulent resistance from Hindu orthodoxy, the duo got Lord William Bentinck to abolish sati in 1829 and make it a criminal offence.

It is almost impossible to conjure up today how big a victory this was in nineteenth-century Bengal. Suffice it to say that it has been consistently mentioned by historians as one of the triggers of the First War of Indian Independence, or The Sepoy Mutiny as the British describe it, less than three decades later in 1857.

"The abolition of sati, the abolition of infanticide, the intro-duction of vaccination, the law to legalise the remarriage of Hindu widows...were pressed upon the attention of the army and the masses as so many deliberate attacks on the outworks of Mahom-medanism and Hinduism," wrote Sir William Lee-Warner in *Life of the Marquis of Dalhousie* (1904).[2]

"And the simple, superstitious, credulous sepoys were told that the time was rapidly approaching when by some piece of jadu (magic) the Christians would...uncaste the whole Hindu popula-tion and outrage all their traditions and feelings."

The second part of the quotation is mostly the figment of colo-nial imagination that sees colonial rule as the advancement of the natives and the "white man's burden," but the abolition of sati caused a tectonic shift in the power structure of conservative, and at that time as now, majority Hindu society.

But India's merchants, traders and entrepreneurs were forcing societal change even long before Dwarkanath. In 1669, Mughal

Emperor Aurangzeb was at the height of his proselytizing reign. By his orders, numerous Hindu and Jain temples were being destroyed. Faced with the destruction of their places of worship in Surat, and perhaps even their own forced conversion to Islam, Bhimji Parekh, one of the city's wealthiest merchants, took charge.

He complained to the local British trade representative, Gerald Aungier, who was president of the Surat factory—he would in 1672 become the third governor of Bombay—that unless their faith and places of worship were protected, most of the merchants, the backbone of trade in Surat, would leave en masse for Bombay.

Makrand Mehta writes in his 1991 book *Indian Merchants and Entrepreneurs in Historical Perspective* that this left the Englishman torn. He sympathized with Bhimji, but letting the merchants go would mostly likely result in the eruption of the military wrath of the Mughals against the British. He couldn't risk that.

But he didn't want to offend the powerful merchant clans, so he told Bhimji that Bombay was not yet fortified enough to guard the merchants and their families. He suggested that "hereafter as occasion offered, they with more ease and security convey their estates and families to Bombay by degrees where they might assure themselves of all favour, friendship and freedom in their religion and encouragement in their trade as they could in reason [expect] from us."[3]

This was no time for, in Mehta's words, a "post-dated cheque." So on September 23 and 24, 1669, more than 8,000 merchant families left Surat for Bharaoch in Bombay.

"The general strike followed by the merchants' flight created such a tense atmosphere in Surat that the political authorities were forced to change their stand. The *banias* returned to Surat on December 20, 1669 only after the state assured the safety of their religion."

As Mehta notes, this was not only the first-ever mercantile strike in India, it was also entirely nonviolent.

Not content to fight only the social ill of religious prejudice, 30 years later Surat's merchants gathered to fight corrupt governance. In 1702, the governor of Surat and his partner in crime, a trader called Ahmad Chelaby, took Rs 85,000 from the *banias*, ostensibly to help defend the city against Maratha marauders. When they realized that they had been cheated, the merchants went on strike, lowering their shutters and forcing the administration to imprison Chelaby and return at least Rs 37,000.

The idea that entrepreneurs—business people—can collaborate and push forward social reform is now lost in the venal crony capitalism of large portions of big business of India. Indian entrepreneurs seek tax benefits and reach out to manipulate laws to make windfall gains on land deals, but social reform does not, for the most part, keep them awake.

Some of this disconnect comes from the late years of the independence movement against the British Raj. Even though Mahatma Gandhi had deep and enduring friendships with top entrepreneurs like the Birla family, the overall ties of the Congress Party, which led the independence movement, with entrepreneurs never went very deep.

The historian Claude Markovits makes this point in his excellent book *Merchants, Traders, Entrepreneurs: Indian Business in the Colonial Era.* He points out that Indian Marxist historical writing, often the dominant point of view, "stresses the limitations of the Indian bourgeoisie without treating it as compradore."[4]

He writes:

For these (Marxist) authors, the bourgeoisie could establish only a limited hegemony over the national movement, given an alliance with propertied elements in the countryside. The concept of "passive revolution," borrowed by these authors from Gramsci, by which they define the Indian freedom struggle, serves to emphasize that neither the masses, in spite of their mobilization, nor the bourgeoisie, because of its own weakness, could give the national movement a clear direction for the radical transformation of the country either in a capitalist or socialist direction. The process was basically one of limiting popular initiative and maintaining the movement within limits that objectively suited bourgeois interests.

Markovits says there are two problems with this reasoning. First, the Indian bourgeoisie barely existed as a defined class in pre-1947 (before independence) India, and the relationship between economics and politics in Italy was very different from the relationship between economics and politics in India.

In India, the dominant ideology—which still had a powerful hold on the minds of even the members of the westernized elite—treated the economy as a simple function of the social and political order, and not as an autonomous domain. The attitude of the Congress leaders to Indian capitalists must be placed within this context. They believed in the primacy of politics over economics and therefore did not attach much importance to the precise nature of the economic regime of an independent India. They thought that the economy would somehow "follow" and that once the fetters of foreign domination were removed, it would become robust.

It is this kind of loose nonchalance and lack of engagement that has, in some sense, led to the disconnect that exists today, so much so that in the 2014 elections, prominent political leaders regularly bashed the country's top businessmen as corrupt and venal (sometimes quite correctly).

Markovits points out that this pre-independence unease still echoes 60 years later. "Is it not possible to see in institutionalized corruption, the financing of political parties, especially the ruling party, by business houses, and state financial support to private 'monopolies,' the modern equivalents of the farming of tax revenue or of the granting of state monopolies to private firms?"

This is why, in a sense, enterprise and social change so diverged in modern India. The tale of enterprise has been divorced from the larger sociopolitical tale of India—this is partly because some of the most successful entrepreneurial tales of the liberalization period that began in 1991, like the information technology (IT) companies such as Infosys, happened far away from the usual shenanigan-filled world of India Inc. (the term used to describe the aggregation of business houses in India). In fact, one prominent government minister even used to joke that the IT companies could grow swiftly because the government didn't know much about them in their early years of the 1990s and 2000s.

This is the story of that enterprise of the *aam aadmi*. India is unlikely to have a cohesive spring of revolt. How can we, in a country where land area under Maoist rebel control and shopping malls often rise simultaneously? What we are having is a daily climatic noon, somewhere in this vast nation, the total of V. S. Naipaul's "million mutinies." Except that it might not always be a mutiny but—that curious reality TV term—a makeover.

But who are these mutineers? Consider this: India's 7,000 biggest companies employ only around 7 percent of its workforce.

The remaining 93 percent come from what is called the "unorganized sector," a euphemism that straddles all the worlds from a roadside tea shop to a small diamond-polishing unit. There are about 30 million such units in India, each employing an average of seven people. This is the backbone of the Indian economy—reflected not in the stock markets but in the kitchens and keenness of aspiration in millions of homes.

There are those who still hope for a China-style mass-manufacturing revolution in India. That is unlikely for many reasons—from disjointed, disparate landownership in India to family-run firms that lack capital or manpower to scale up. But something else is happening in India. Its village economy, which is home to 68 percent of the population and which brings in 50 percent of the GDP, is transforming. What was an income pyramid in 2010—with 50 million people earning more than $5 a day at the pointed tip, 350 million making between $1 and $5, and 400 million scraping by on less than $1 a day—is estimated to chisel itself into a diamond shape by 2020. This means 150 million people earning more than $5 a day, a fat rhombus middle of 500 million people making between $1 and $5 a day and 250 million taking in less than $1 a day.

This means 150 million first-time consumers of everything from more nutritious food to better soaps. This means 150 million first-time consumers of "brands" in a country where most of the poor and especially the rural poor buy "loose" unpackaged goods.

Already most people working in village or small-town India do not get their income from agriculture—only 40 percent do. The rest have found work in everything from local retail to local banking and small-scale manufacturing. In a sense, millions of people have found, and are finding, new enterprises. The best definition I

have heard of an entrepreneur in my ten years as a business journalist came from a village teacher in the dusty district of Alwar
in India's western desert state of Rajasthan. I met him about two
years ago during a stop at a tea stall in the middle of nowhere
on the road from Alwar to Delhi. I am ashamed to say that I do
not remember his name, but what he said has echoed in me ever
since. "An entrepreneur is not only a businessman as all you town
people think," said the school teacher. "Anyone who makes his
life and the place, the world around him better is an entrepreneur.
We have millions of women in the villages of India who keep the
villages going. Each one of them is an entrepreneur. It is because
of them that nothing collapses. They hold things up."[5]

*It is because of them that nothing collapses. They hold things
up.* I had never heard a better description of the ideal entrepreneur. Back in Delhi, I went to meet Pradeep Kashyap, who has
built India's finest rural research organization, MART. When we
met one September morning at his quiet office in the middle of
Noida's industrial zone, amid factories and ferries just on the outskirts of the Indian capital, he seemed angry. "There is an explosion in work and consumer demand in rural India and yet at the
same time there is a raging Maoist revolution that runs through
almost a third of the country—doesn't that sound crazy?" said
Kashyap.

It is that odd truth about India—ostensibly the same demo-
graphic, a broad swath of rural India, is revolting and retailing
at the same time. In fact, some of the Indian states most affected
by Communist rebel violence are also some of the fastest-growing
economies in India. This is a war for, and not against, prosperity.

Were it not for the steady increase, however modest, in prosperity and aspiration—as desolately tragic as some of the worst
neglected, hunger-prone areas are—the violence would be many

times more vicious. And quite possibly there would be no India, only a broken smattering of balkanized, quarreling states.

It is this rise of the common entrepreneur that keeps the idea of India afloat. But modern India does not celebrate the common entrepreneur. It celebrates billionaires, sometimes even barely disguised oligarchs, while neglecting to applaud these everyday miracles of enterprise that glue it together.

This proliferation of entrepreneurs is not happening in isolation. The government has launched several large schemes that created what I call a "rights economy." A rights economy is one in which the state commits to deliver several services to the citizens—such as a minimum amount of food to those who cannot afford it and health care—not just as welfare but as a guaranteed legal right. This, in turn has created a new universe of empowered consumers and micro-entrepreneurs.

I first realized this at Kotkasim, about a two-hour drive from Alwar, Rajasthan, where Jaisingh Vyas told me about Paanch Bhai soap. Vyas ran a grocery in the district where the government launched a pilot scheme in 2012 to transfer kerosene oil subsidies to the poor directly as cash. Money was deposited into the bank accounts of the area's 25,000 people who hold below-poverty-line (BPL, a government measure for low-income groups that need state dole) cards, for them to buy kerosene at market rates. Subsidized kerosene costs Rs 15 a liter (about a quart) in ration shops and around Rs 50 in the open market. The government pays BPL card holders Rs 35 for a liter, in effect the difference. Each person has a monthly quota of three liters.

Two things happened after the scheme was introduced: one, an entire supply of 84,000 liters (about 22,190 gallons) of kerosene, earlier ostensibly sold on paper, dropped to 22,000 liters (about 5,812 gallons). Second, only half the BPL card holders could get themselves a bank account (to receive cash transfers) because of bureaucratic delays, lack of banking staff, and the inability of the poorly educated card holders to grasp banking paperwork. Although the scheme's results highlighted India's usual problems of corruption and implementation, it was still a success. Cash transfers have been rolled out in 25 schemes across 121 districts and have impacted around 10 percent of the population ever since.

But what's this got to do with soap? Vyas tells me that many buyers of Paanch Bhai are beneficiaries of the kerosene cash transfers. "People hear all the time through government campaigns that soap needs to be used to stay healthy. So when they get some money, soap is one of the main things they buy." Sales at his tiny shop have gone up from one or two bars of soap to four or five every day.

Another program inadvertently bolstered the trend. Between 2004 and 2012, the Congress-led government built 93,426 toilets under the Nirmal Bharat Abhiyan (NBA), its flagship program that aims to drastically reduce the number of Indians without access to toilets. As much as 50 percent of the country's population defecates in the open, but that's down from about 75 percent two decades ago.

This push for better sanitation, coupled with the cash transfer, is something that makes Desh Bandhu Madan happy. His family owns the Paanch Bhai (or Five Brothers) brand, which was started by his father and uncles in 1957. With six factories in Faridabad, each of which had a turnover of Rs 24 crore in 2012, Madan and his brothers have captured most of what he calls the *pehli baar*, or first-time customers for the soap in Haryana, Rajasthan, Punjab, Himachal Pradesh, Uttar Pradesh, Gujarat, and Jammu and Kashmir.

Paanch Bhai is value for money. At Rs 44 a kilogram (about 2.2 pounds), wrapped in yellow wax paper, it is one of the cheapest branded soaps here. Premium products such as Wheel or Rin from Hindustan Unilever sell at around Rs 50 for 160 grams (about 5.6 ounces). Madan says demand for Paanch Bhai has been growing at more than 10 percent each year for the last three years. Each factory sells 550 metric tons (606 short tons) of soap a month. Still, demand outstrips production by at least 50 percent.

"You have to understand who buys my soap," explains Madan. It's the village woman who has been using ash to clean up for a long time until she learns of government campaigns and goes to buy the soap. Washing soap ubiquitously doubles as hand soap in this market.

Much like India's "rights-based governance system," a "rights-based economy" is at work here.

Economists have always debated the social and economic aspects of India's roughly Rs 190,000 crore annual spending on social welfare schemes, such as the Mahatma Gandhi National Rural Employment Guarantee Act (MNREGA) and the Sarva Siksha Abhiyan (SSA), which promises free primary schooling. But few have examined the impact of all that money through the lens of rising purchasing power, mostly in rural India. Experts say that nearly two decades of economic growth and the last ten years of sustained government spending have fueled a unique transformation in many villages.

What the soap example shows is that when subsidies move from kind to cash, beneficiaries find the best use for it, often in areas that the state wouldn't have thought of (less kerosene, more soap). Schemes like MNREGA fuel the rights economy by putting cash directly into the hands of beneficiaries, while programs like SSA allow the poor to redirect the money they would otherwise have spent on their children's schooling.

It's very difficult to ascertain the size of the rights economy. For one, there are still enough leakages to distort the picture. Also, it's not a part of the rural economy as we know it, but a subset of it. No study has been done—it is perhaps not even possible—to demarcate which part of the new purchasing power of the poor came from GDP–led growth (fueling the rural economy), and which resulted from social welfare schemes. Often, the lines between them blur. But there is enough evidence that the two are now going hand in hand to effect the economic change seen across India's villages, where around 68 percent of the country's population lives.

When C. K. Prahalad wrote his seminal book *The Fortune at the Bottom of the Pyramid: Eradicating Poverty through Profits* in 2004, he argued that companies would discover a huge market if they built products targeting the purchasing power of the poor by seeking out an existing market and fixing the supply side.

What makes the rights economy different—and why it's attractive to companies—is that it's spawning a new level of demand. When people who have rarely, if ever, had disposable income get access to hard cash, what they choose to buy, even if in small quantities, forms the heart of this economy. It's often driven by people who aspire to surpass their relatively poor rural neighbor's purchasing power and buy an expensive product, say a bottle of Coke or Pepsi, instead of three cups of tea at the roadside stall. Indeed, one way of looking at the rights economy is as an aggregation of splurges.

"When the poor get cash, they spend it exactly the same way as us—on private education or private health care and food, from subsistence level to fruits and vegetables and meat," says economist Surjit S. Bhalla, refuting the notion that the poor spend differently from the middle class. (Bhalla also believes that most of the subsidies don't reach the beneficiaries.) He cites the experience of Santiago Levy, father of the cash transfer system in Mexico in the mid-1990s. Levy, who was undersecretary in the Treasury Department when he proposed the cash transfer plan, had famously asked: "Once you realise that all you are transferring is income, the obvious question is why you don't just give them income directly." The success of income transfer was seen in two pilot projects in Madhya Pradesh between June 2011 and January 2012. Conducted by the charity organizations SEWA Bharat and UNICEF, 6,000 people across two villages were given Rs 300 per adult and Rs 150 per child with no restrictions on spending it. The main items they bought were better education for children, better walls, better food, roofs for their homes and toilets.

For Madurai-based Manickam Ramaswami, managing director of Rs 1,500 crore Loyal Textiles, there's a "forced trickle-down" benefit. He cites a survey done by his industry a year after the MNREGA was implemented in 2006. It showed a 26 percent rise in the purchase of textiles among BPL families. What happened was that he used to get his low cost labor from rural areas. But with the introduction of MNREGA, the cost of this labor had to increase because the workers now had a choice to stay in their village, instead of working in the textile factory in the town, and earn the same amount of money. So wages had to rise. "What we were paying our workers—Rs 60 a day—was below subsistence. But I could not have unilaterally raised pay, because competition would price me out. The MNREGA made the market equal for everyone." Today he pays a minimum wage of Rs 180 a day.

Kashyap of MART talks of how often he sees an empty pack of Dove soap lying in a village room. "It says we are not left behind." Sales of the premium Unilever soap are growing rapidly in rural India. Kashyap points out that the country's social sector spending, depending on the year, could easily match or exceed the approximate annual turnover of its soaps, clothes and food industry (Rs. 170,000 crore), and its contribution to aspiration and consumption is underrated.

He believes there are a few factors responsible for this. One, most people living in villages no longer till the land. Farming accounts for only 40 percent of the rural economy (some call it the rural GDP). Manufacturing is 20 percent, and the bulk of that is low-skill, including traditional crafts and artifacts, and services like rural retail make up for the rest. The other factors are migration from villages to towns and cities, reach of mass media, and ever-improving connectivity between villages and cities, for instance via all-weather roads and cities like Delhi or Bombay expanding into ever-intermingling city-villages. "When people talk of direct cash transfers, I say there is also direct culture transfer that is happening rapidly from urban to rural India, where urban habits are quickly picked up and adopted."

Economist Sudipto Mundle, formerly with the Asian Development Bank, points to another factor: he says that compared to the middle class, the poor have the maximum propensity to spend (and conversely, the least to save), when given the opportunity.

All of this is leading to a reexamination of the alleged rich-poor or urban-rural divide. According to Pratap Bhanu Mehta, president of the Centre for Policy Research, the country's leading think tank, "This Bharat vs. India—what is good for rich India is not good for the poor—divide does not hold anymore. Bharat and India are far more interlinked through domestic migration, remittances, formal and informal labour, and endless feedback loops than people can think of. What is happening is a combination of growth and government spending."

This is best illustrated by Vivek Puri, who runs Puri Oil Mills, whose P Mark mustard oil is one of the strongest players in Jammu and Kashmir, Ladakh, Punjab, Himachal Pradesh, and Haryana. His annual turnover is Rs 250 crore. "My grandfather [who started the company in 1933] and father would talk about how people use mustard oil for body massage across India. Five years ago, I realised the trend was dying even in villages. Young people don't like mustard oil for massage. It is too sticky and pungent, and not in the least fashionable," says Puri.

He hired scientists to experiment with other formulas, and the result was Shakti, a perfumed light oil for massage, which comes in 100 milliliter (about 3.4 fluid ounce) bottles for Rs 50. However, he also innovated by making the packaging dowdy. "Most of our buyers are women who live with their in-laws, and while they want to buy a superior product, they don't want to be seen spending money on a fancy cosmetic product." The slightly shabby packaging helps them buy Shakti oil and yet not get into trouble at home. Demand for Shakti has been growing at 8 percent annually.

Social scientist and author Dipankar Gupta, who has spent 40 years studying the rural markets, however, says it's wrong to term these people consumers. "The increase in purchasing power doesn't make them consumers," he says, adding that a consumer is someone who buys things purely out of desire. This is, at best, an increase in purchasing power for a few, and the items bought are matters of dire necessity. He adds that the government's ability to stop the theft of money spent on social projects will be critical to the increase in purchasing power. States that govern the best, like Kerala, may see the highest impact.

So what does this new phenomenon do to conventional business? One, it will challenge consumer goods companies' classic market segmentation by population, income and education. Nikhil Joshi, managing director of Sapat Tea, a company that operates only in Maharashtra, is aware of this challenge. He uses 12,000 marketing agents, which gives him immense insight into how consumers think. To sell one of his labels, Sahyadri Tea, in Vidharbha three years ago, he realized that just pricing things cheaper than the competition would not work. "Though the people were very poor, they wanted to buy something different and get the satisfaction of buying something better than usual." Pitched as an extra-strong tea, Sahyadri now sells at a premium of roughly Rs 5 over other brands (Tata Agni, Assam Dust) for a 250-gram (about 8.8-ounce) pack and is growing at 20 percent annually.

Or take the example of Rajkot-based Chandubhai Virani's Rs 1,000 crore chips and snacks empire, Balaji Wafers. Virani sells wafers for Rs 5 a packet. Balaji has 90 percent of the market in Gujarat, and by some estimates more than 75 percent in western India. Seven Balaji plants process 5 lakh (1 lakh = 100,000) kilograms (more than a million pounds) each of potatoes and pulses every day. It's the second-biggest player in this category with 14 percent of all-India market share. Virani says 70 percent of his revenue comes from the lowest-priced items, targeted at people "who need to eat cheap, quickly, and what fills their stomach and does not make them ill." He travels through construction sites and villages every week to see if people are buying Balaji. One trick he employs to keep his costs low: he uses zero advertising.

Virani, who started out as a canteen boy at a local film theater in Dhundoraji, about 80 kilometers (about 50 miles) from Rajkot, says "part of the demand comes from a giant sociological leap." He argues that villagers earlier thought of packaged foods as stale. "Now the idea of bacteria is understood by everyone, even by BPL customers. Something sealed in a packet is considered safe," he says, adding, "Anyone can open a Rs 10 pack of chips from any international company and one of our Rs 5 packs, and see if there is any difference in quality." (According to a Nielsen study, in 2011 more than 58 percent of Indian demand for salty snacks came from rural India.) Then, as an aside Virani says that for the past year, Pepsi (makers of Frito Lay) has been aggressively trying to buy a 25 percent stake in his company, but he has not yet agreed.

Adi Godrej, chairman and managing director of Godrej Industries, is a strong supporter of the MNREGA. He thinks it is good because it is creating millions of new potential customers, and he believes that companies should focus on having products ready for them. "Only in three things there is full penetration—toilet soap, detergent and matchsticks. In everything else, there is a long way to go to even get awareness going," says Godrej. Thirty-five percent of his sales already come from rural India.

Biraj Patanaik, principal advisor to the Supreme Court Commissioners on Food, says industry must realize that it is rural demand that saved India during the 2008 crisis. "A lot of it was helped by the MNREGA." He echoes Godrej when he adds that the government is helping India Inc. by creating millions of empowered future customers for them through rights governance.

However, the rights-based economy still has a long way to go. Yamini Aiyar, whose Accountability Initiative is India's only organization that tracks grassroots government spending, says this kind of demand has barely scratched the surface because of the lack of delivery mechanisms. "The trouble is that we don't have the district-level, or block-level people to enforce government schemes, including cash transfers." She rues the fact that we keep talking about technology, but on the ground people can barely use pen and paper correctly. Rights governance, coupled with rural economic growth, is waiting to fuel an explosion of demand. But industry needs to push for administrative reforms and provide better training to tap it. "What they would be doing is securing a very large future market," says Aiyar.

In such an environment, many *aam* entrepreneurs are targeting some of the most protracted problems of the Indian nation-state. For one, they are moving India from a reactive to a responsive democracy. To understand this simply, think of the old Bollywood Hindi film where the cops would always arrive late. That was the usual pace of the Indian state—if they arrived at all.

But the expansion of India's grassroots enterprise means that an unprecedented tide of daily pressure is being brought to bear on the delivery mechanisms of the state. An empowered, entrepreneurial citizenry is ready to exert pressure not merely in one riotous burst, but in a relentless daily campaign to chip away at the malevolent resistance of feudal politics and fetid bureaucracy.

International conglomerates have always smiled happily at the thought of India's millions of new consumers, especially in the middle class, and the late author and management guru C. K. Prahalad spoke about the fortune at the bottom of the pyramid. But to see Indian society today merely as a mass of consumers is perhaps fundamentally flawed.

India is fast becoming a nation of creators as well as consumers. Indeed, it's in this mushrooming of latent creativity that India's redemption likely lies. Looking for the next "Arab Spring" is the new pastime of the West, but it might find a different season in India, where the high noon of dissent cleanses the ills of democracy not with a sudden war but rather with an incessant, intelligent wearing down.

As I started writing this book, I met Chandra Bhan Prasad, a prominent intellectual in India who writes on his community, the Dalits, long considered untouchables in orthodox Hinduism, and the impact of capitalism on the community. He laughed when I asked him what his answer was to those who ask when the revolution would come to India.

"It has already come. It has happened. Only we are a very large country and you might not see it everywhere yet but the revolution has happened and all the upper-caste intellectuals and Brahmins have never bothered to notice," Prasad guffawed. "But how will they? Many of the so-called great Marxists of India were upper-caste land owners and then they became Marxists and started declaring what the poor and the oppressed need. They had no clue."

Enterprise and consumer demand at the grassroots level are completely transforming centuries-old social barriers, says Prasad. He is from Azamgarh in eastern Uttar Pradesh, notorious, sometimes unfairly, for seeding Islamic terror. These are the areas of north India that foreign journalists sometimes describe as the "badlands" of the country. In such areas, the battle between the Dalits and other low castes and the upper-caste Bhumihars, Thakurs and Brahmins has gone on for generations, and always with blood-soaked attacks and reprisals.

Prasad tells me a tale of change. The first is from a village in eastern Uttar Pradesh on the Jaunpur-Azamgarh road. The number of bullocks in the village dropped from 1,200 to 4 between 1995 and 2005. You might think this is a natural transition from animal plowing to machine plowing. But Prasad found a deeper reason. There was no one to plow with the animals any more. "This was a task done traditionally by the lower castes, the upper castes would not do this because it involved taking care of the animals, working with dung, all of which the upper-caste landlord wouldn't do," said Prasad. "Landlord after landlord complained to me that the Dalits have left the village and moved to the city with better jobs. Once they taste the city life, no one wants to return to this kind of work in the village. No matter how much money they are given. There had been no choice but to get machines. The entire working relationship between the Thakurs and Bhumihars and the Dalits has broken down. What do you think this mobility, this migration represents to the Dalits? Is it not enterprise?"

This tale of dramatic social change brought about by commerce and enterprise is best captured in a Prasad phrase: "Pizza delivery *ka koi jaath nahin hota*" (Pizza delivery has no caste).

Empowered by urban anonymity and commerce, Dalits across India are tearing down centuries of bizarre and bloody repression. In 2010, Prasad was part of a four-member team, including Devesh Kapur, the director of the Center for the Advanced Study of India at the University of Pennsylvania; Lant Prichett, from the Kennedy School of Government at Harvard University; and D. Shyam Babu, of the Rajeev Gandhi Institute for Contemporary Studies, that studied all Dalit households (19,087) in two districts of Uttar Pradesh (Bilaria Ganj in the Azamgarh district from the east and Khurja from the Bulandshahar district from the west) to compare their lives before and after Indian economic liberalization, from 1990 to 2008.

What they found startled them. There had been a sea change in the number of Dalits owning consumer items, like bicycles, fans, TVs and mobile phones, and living in concrete houses.

On average, in both areas, roughly 50 percent more people started living in concrete homes in this period of economic growth; the number of TV set owners grew by 33 percent; 45 percent more households had fans; and of course mobile phone ownership had jumped, from near zero to almost 35 percent of the households. Just to get a sense of how impoverished the situation used to be—for the first time, a quarter of households in both areas had chairs.

There was an even more intimate transformation. Few people here had ever used toothpaste. This number jumped a combined average of more than 65 percent. Shampoo use, another unheard-of luxury, jumped nearly 70 percent.

What impact did this have on centuries of discrimination during which it was forbidden to drink water from a glass touched by a Dalit or eat from a plate used by a Dalit?

The instances of upper castes eating and drinking at Dalit homes, once nearly unthinkable, rose more than 70 percent in the east and nearly 45 percent in the west. The practice that only Dalits would pick up dead animals almost disappeared.

"The migrating Dalit worker picked up more money than ever at jobs at the nearest town or city and changed their habits and society forever," said Prasad. He says that to understand what changed, it is not the Dalit who should be asked, but the upper castes.

"I remember this Bhumihar landlord in eastern Uttar Pradesh telling me that, '*Aaj kal uhi log lal murgi haath mein pakar ke motorbike mein pharphareke jaate hain*' [These days these people buy plump red chicken and pass by our houses holding the fluttering birds and zipping by on their motorbikes]! His resentment and disappointment was utterly complete, and the whole thing was very funny for me," laughs Prasad. "Earlier social rank was by birth alone, but now status could be bought by enterprise—that is a priceless change."

And this change was not restricted to Uttar Pradesh. In Sangli, in the western state of Maharashtra, he asked an upper-caste Patil woman why she was working on the large farm of a successful Dalit food manufacturer.

She told him that earlier the *tulsi* plant (considered sacred and to be found only in the front yards of the upper caste) defined who you were. Now it's whether you have a TV or not. "I don't think of this as a farm," she said. "This is so big, and all the rules are like a factory. A factory has no caste."

This is the revolution, Prasad told me—don't look for Tahrir Square or the guillotine. It is happening every single day.

When I told my mother all this, as always she had something to add. "See, all this enterprise-shenterprise, na, this is why I taught you to make bread and butter and omelet when you were only ten years old," she said. "You must be free. Not like your father. Totally not free. Who is going to cook and feed you? All that is gone. Mother is the last woman doing that. No wife these days. If you can't even feed yourself every day, what freedom?"

Even my mother seemed to understand that our regular, every-day rebellion—enterprise—is what sets us free.

CHAPTER 2

BUSINESS MODELS IN THE WORLD'S MOST DANGEROUS PLACE

"If we delay you," says the English and Urdu sign on the gate, "for more than two hours, we will pay you Rs 2 per minute for every extra minute."

This is one of the first things that a driver carrying a truckload of apples—anywhere between 50 apples and a ton of apples—sees when he arrives at the gate of the cold storage and fruit processing factory of Harshna Naturals in Lassipura district. The factory is about an hour and a half's drive north from Srinagar, the capital of Jammu and Kashmir.

The man who put up the sign, 31-year-old agriculture entrepreneur Khurram Mir, says the sign works like a talisman, telling the farmers who come to sell and store fruits at his plant, his workers and even himself that things are getting better in a valley in which, depending on who you are reading, between 50,000 and 100,000 people have been killed in a two-decade insurgency that started in 1989.

"We are saying yes, things are so normal that we can pay for delays in a state used to shutting down for days with violence and anxiety." Once described (by former US president Bill Clinton) as the world's most dangerous place, this is the new sign of peace in Jammu and Kashmir, the Himalayan state over which India and Pakistan have fought three wars.

Long used to peace brokers in the shape of politicians, diplomats, aid workers, even ex-militants, the valley is getting used to a new kind of agent of calm: the entrepreneur.

And why not? More small and medium enterprises have been set up in Kashmir in the last two years than in the previous decade, says the Jammu and Kashmir Entrepreneurship Development Institute (JKEDI).[1] Its two flagship projects have produced more than 1,700 new entrepreneurs in the last two years, says Zamir Qadri, head of the JKEDI. One project provides unemployed high school graduates with 35 percent of the cost of their dream project or Rs 3 lakhs, whichever sum is lower, with the remaining amount financed as a loan by the Jammu and Kashmir Bank, the biggest bank in the region. The amount for postgraduates is 35 percent of the project cost or Rs 5 lakhs; and for professionals, Rs 7.5 lakhs. The other project, financed by the National Minorities Development Finance Corporation, gives out loans of an average of Rs 2.5 lakhs to jobless young Kashmiris.

It's a small number, 1,700 entrepreneurs, in a state of 12 million with more than 600,000 registered unemployed people, but Qadri says the numbers are like Mir's signboard—a small step in the right direction that has many people excited. "One of our big problems is that people feel lost—we have lost a generation to the violence. This is one way to tell people that all is not lost and they can start afresh."

Back at the farm in Lassipura, Khurram Mir says the whole idea of new entrepreneurship is about people regaining respect and control of their own lives in a state that is estimated to have more than 330,000 military and paramilitary troops.

"There has been a respect deficit in the state. For instance, no one has ever appreciated the time of the farmer. The power was always in the hands of the people who were buying from the farmer. With this small board, right at the point of entry, we are saying 'you are important' to the farmer," says Mir, who started Harshna Naturals in 2008 after returning from America with a management degree from Purdue University. His father is one of the biggest fruit and vegetable traders in the region. "Basically I came back and told him, 'Dad, I am starting a project that will put you out of business,'" smiles Mir. "And he said, 'Well, we can always find other business opportunities but if the farmers continue to suffer, the state has no future. So best of luck to you.' That was all I needed."

The first Rs 4 crores of investment built 5,000 metric tons (5,512 short tons) of capacity cold storage and a fruit sorting facility. Mir is now aiming to touch 40,000 metric-ton (44,092 short-ton) capacity at the cost of more than Rs 250 crore by 2014. He says there is no dearth of investors since Kashmir is one of the main production hubs for fruits in India with, for instance, 57 percent of the apple production of the country (1.8 million metric tons [1.98 million short tons] in 2010–2011).

But conservative estimates suggest that between 10 percent and 30 percent (in some seasons as high as 45 percent) of the Kashmiri apple crop gets wasted due to the lack of storage and processing facilities in the state, and the farmer is poorer for it. "The farmer has always had to sell when the trader tells him to—this has always been the way in Kashmir. But with the right storage facilities, the power shifts back to the farmer. He can choose when he wants to sell."

To show that his efforts are bearing fruit, Mir forks out a set of charts that display how farmers are taking to Harshna. There are three kinds of business that Harshna is involved in: the company buys produce from farmers to stock and then sell at a later date; multinationals and big corporate houses like Reliance Fresh and Bharti Walmart use its cold storage facilities when they buy from local farmers; and local farmers themselves use the facilities.

The vision statement of Harshna Naturals says that the aim of the company is to be used almost wholly by local farmers. They are certainly moving in that direction. In 2008–2009, big companies used more than 60 percent of Harshna's facilities, while 30 percent was used in-house and only around 10 percent by the local farmers.

In 2012–2013, however, the company did not use any of its facilities to buy and store for itself, exiting that aspect of the business entirely. Less than 30 percent of the space was used by big companies and more than 70 percent by local farmers.

This has also meant that Mir's other big poster—warning that no one should be seen eating an apple within the compound—is taken very seriously these days. "If somebody is seen eating an apple, and there are farmers around, they will immediately wonder, 'Whose apple is that?' And they raise the alarm. We are working to create an environment of full transparency, which has been difficult here." Kashmir was ranked among the four most corrupt states in India in a 2008 Transparency International study; Mir says modern enterprise and systems are bringing sociological change.

"For instance, Kashmiris have always been called lazy, but in 2010, when the stone pelting was going on through the day, what we did was we just did all the work at night!" laughs Mir. "We told our employees that instead of working during the day, just work at night and that way our trucks could pass undisturbed."[2] In a state that has lost five years of working days to strikes in the last 23 years, such innovation is critical. "Today in Kashmir, if there is a will, there is a highway of enterprise that is open," says Mir, who tells his employees that they should never aim to work at Harshna for more than two years. "My standard introduction is—after two years, if you do not leave me and start your own business, then I have failed."

There are many signs that this time around, the peace wave might be enterprise driven. On the back of record tourist arrivals (1.1 million in 2011–2012), Congress Party general secretary

Rahul Gandhi, a personal friend of state chief minister Omar Abdullah, made a gesture in October 2012 that was as much political as it was economic. He invited some of India's biggest tycoons, including Ratan Tata, Kumaramangalam Birla, Deepak Parekh and Rahul Bajaj, to visit the valley with him, promising to bring India's biggest business houses to the beleaguered region. Part of the idea was old—integrating the valley into the economic growth story of India—but as a top-ranking bureaucrat in the Kashmir government told me, the method was new.

"We have tried everything from interlocutors to prime minis-terial missions. Now the thought is the delivery of hope cannot be just top-down. It has to be bottom-up too," said the bureaucrat. "Sometimes economics can tell people that there is something to look forward to better than politics."

Khurram Mir was at a closed-door meeting with the business leaders. "Mr. Birla said for enterprise to grow, there has to be a degree of stability. But I liked what Mr. Tata said—that the true spirit of enterprise is to circumvent the situation and continue the work, and that ultimately brings peace," he says.

In 2011, Tata's Taj chain of hotels opened their first property in the valley, with an 89-room hotel overlooking the Dal Lake and Asia's largest tulip garden and boasting a 2,500-square-foot presi-dential suite. One of the earliest big hotel chains in the valley, The Lalit Group, announced in 2012 that their palace hotel in Srinagar had become the chain's highest revenue generating property after years of losses since they took it over. In 2012 Srinagar's first radio taxi service, called Snow Cabs, was launched, and Kashmir Univer-sity started to offer its first MBA course.

Numbers back Tata's claim. According to the Home Ministry, terrorism-related murders in the valley in 2010–2011 amounted to 2.77 per 100,000 population, lower than the murder rate in

Delhi (3.1) and Haryana (4.1). Essentially many more people are being murdered in the seemingly peaceful heart of India than in what is often described as "insurgency infested" Kashmir. So there is greater consensus than ever that Kashmir's military force needs to be drastically reduced, and a sense that that might be work in progress (the Home Ministry is reviewing a strong proposal) has lifted the mood. One of the big achievements of the Omar Abdullah government has been to keep the army largely in its barracks. For instance, compared to 2004–2005, there are far fewer in-your-face boots on the streets and military check points in Srinagar city. And why not? There is hope from the side of the terrorists too: Syed Sala-huddin, the dreaded chief of the Pakistan-aided Hizbul Mujahideen, declared in 2012 that he has no more men in Kashmir. (In 2014, new threats emerged in Kashmir from ISIS and Al Qaeda, but the push to reduce army presence remains extremely strong and many argue it is key to reducing support for militancy.)

In a valley jaded by talk of violence and talk of peace in equal measure, enterprise-driven peace is a welcome new development. In these years, there have been regular summers of peace with the usual tourist flood and hype in a place where the first signpost outside the airport says "Welcome to paradise on earth," taken from the lines written by the thirteenth-century poet Amir Khus-rau: "*Agar firdous baroye zameen ast; Hami asto, hami asto, hami ast*" (If there is paradise on earth, it is here, it is here, it is here).

In a state that has one of the highest government employee-to-population ratios, with around 500,000 government workers (states of similar size like Jharkhand or Himachal Pradesh have one-fifth the number of state employees), stability among the guns has always meant a government job. Among the state's 350,000 craftsmen families, whose skills have been developed over the centuries, the trend in the last 20 years has been to abandon those skills to hunt for even the lowest-rung posts as a peon or a guard.

That might now be changing.

This is why after 14 months of hard work and an invitation to attend the L'Artigiano, the annual global arts fair in Milan, 29-year-old Arifa Jan still says she has to lead a dual life. A bit like Batman, she laughs.

Jan works to revive Numdah, the eleventh-century rug-making technique said to have been popularized by the Mughal emperor Akbar. Her father is a helper in the state transport department. Both her parents are illiterate.

"Usually Numdah was made by the lower castes, and that's why I can't even tell my relatives what exactly my business is. I just tell them that I am into handicrafts. I can never discuss what I am actually doing," says Jan.

Two years ago she was selected for an unemployed youth training program of the JKEDI, which gives seed capital between Rs 3 and 7.5 lakhs upon completion of training. Jan decided to work with Numdah, which was a dying art form in the valley, with terrible quality and inflated prices. She uses only pure merino wool for her rugs, which cost between Rs 3,200 and Rs 8,500 (the cheap rugs made with cotton come apart in weeks). Of the first lot of 300 pieces that she made, 85 percent were sold immediately. She was also invited to participate in the fests organized by Dastkar, the crafts body in Delhi.

"I feel that there are a lot of things that the world does not know about Kashmir. That's what my business is all about. I want to teach the world about Kashmir," says Jan, who recently got her passport for her first trip outside India (to Milan). Even in India, she has only traveled to Delhi.

To understand what is happening to a state economy where the average annual gross state domestic product has more than doubled—from around $6 billion to more than $13 billion—between 2004 and 2012, listen to Haseeb Drabu, the former chairman of the Jammu and Kashmir (J&K) Bank, who now works as a private consultant in Mumbai.

"There was always a lot of money in the state," says Drabu. "Kashmir has never had the kind of poverty that for instance Bihar or Bengal had with absolute malnutrition. Whether it's from the central government or from vested interests in militancy (including from Pakistan), money has flowed into the state. But now there is a palpable difference. The son of an orchardist is not content to remain just another orchardist. He wants to bring in modern machinery and take it to the next level. Is this one big magical change? No. But you are definitely seeing the beginning of a change in mindset and sociological makeup. People are not leaving everything to the government. They are taking some things into their own hands."

Drabu says a lot of the change also happened with the penetration of the availability of finance. During his tenure from 2005 to 2010 as chairman and CEO of J&K Bank, Drabu changed the lending pattern of the bank from 10 percent to people in the valley and the rest to big companies across India to 60 percent local lending. He says it helped the bank build an almost zero non-performing asset book since "it was hundreds of small loans." It also took the credit deposit ratio (CDR; the ratio between the amount of money a bank holds and the amount it lends) from 20 percent to 62 percent. According to the Reserve Bank of India, a low CDR is usually indicative of tepid entrepreneurial activity. While the CDR has fallen from the heights achieved by Drabu, not least because of the massive slowdown in the Indian economy in the last couple of years, it is still growing year-on-year. According to the latest figures available in March 2013, J&K Bank's CDR rose from 36.14 percent to 39.59 percent between March 2012 and 2013. In the first two quarters of 2014, it showed a surge in CDR to 42.81 percent by March 31, 2014.[3]

One of the numbers that suggest this is the rise of the state's GDP. As Drabu explains, a compounded annual growth rate (CAGR) of 13.2 percent in recent years cannot be only government dole and illicit money.

Fayaz Bhat, 47, took advantage of this growth when he started iQuasar (earlier Musky Software) in 2004. The company now has a turnover of $2 million and 47 employees. His office is at the software development park at Rangreth on the outskirts of Srinagar. He says he fights every day to change the mindset of the people around him, including that of his own father, who was a gauge reader with the state water board. "Even today my father is not happy that I am doing something on my own. If I tell him that my private sector job pays Rs 50,000 and a government job pays Rs 10,000 a month, he will say take the government job," says Bhat who is now COO at iQuasar.

But that's not the only impediment to entrepreneurship. Speaking on Skype from Manhattan, Bhat's partner Tahir Qazi, who is CEO, says their company is a great example of how "India grows at night when the government sleeps." "As Kashmiri entrepreneurs we began with a feeling that we need to make things happen in spite of the problems. For instance, we have never paid one paisa in bribes. Everyone here pays bribes but we just don't. That means we are obstructed at every level by bureaucrats all the time."

A case in point is this Kafkaesque incident: in late 2012 iQuasar received their latest factory license, good for two years, from the Department of Labour and the office of the Chief Inspector of Factories. The license, a copy of which was shown to me, clearly says that it's valid until December 31, 2011.

Only it was signed on September 19, 2012, and sent to the company.

"Now what do I do with this? You tell me," says Bhat with a smile. He says he will keep the license and assume it is for the next two years and only apply again for 2015.

Nearby, at the Essar-owned Aegis BPO (business process outsourcing company), Omar Wani, the manager in charge for Kashmir, says he once had a raid by factory inspectors who accused him of not having a manufacturing license.

"I told them hold on, what am I manufacturing? They said, no, this is a factory. I was like—but you tell me what is being manufactured here? Nothing. They just didn't understand what a BPO does but wanted bribes. So I was determined, you fine me, shut me down and I will go to court and fight for as long as it takes." Faced with aggression, the inspectors backed off and after a few days cleared the BPO.

Wani says he is able to face this kind of harassment because of the enthusiasm his employees show. Of approximately 200 people between the ages of 19 and 27 years who work at the BPO, most leave in about two to three years, almost always to start their own enterprise.

"There have been people who have started a shop, become a trader, all sorts of things. You see, what they lack is a purpose, a sense of confidence. Here's what I think we do. We don't run a BPO at all. We run a service where young people come to be told that they too can make it in life, that they too have it in them. Once they have that, they can fend for themselves. The demand for government service has come from the fact that people had very low expectations of themselves and that was the ultimate comfort zone."

I asked the question about bribing for licenses when I met the chief minister of Jammu and Kashmir, Omar Abdullah. At 42, Abdullah is one of the youngest chief ministers in India and is seen as a potential reformer in a state where more than 60 percent of the population is under 30 years of age.

The BlackBerry-carrying chief minister, wearing a navy blue track suit (rather than the kurta pajama that politicians prefer, especially when meeting the press) since he had just returned from a walk, grimaced. "A license? Which company did you say?" It seemed that he was making a mental note. "This is exactly why we pushed through a Public Service Guarantee Act last year," said Abdullah. "It takes a bit of time to spread to every department, but this is now monitored directly by my office."

The Public Service Guarantee Act, now implemented by eight Indian states, makes the delivery of a set of essential services, from the connection of electricity to—as in the case of Kashmir—industrial license renewal, a public service, the denial of which is a criminal offence.

"The idea is that, for instance, we train young entrepreneurs and they come out and cannot get licenses and clearances without paying bribes. These cases come straight to the entrepreneurship development body and then straight to the chief minister's office. We take action and I am personally reviewing these things."

This seems to be true, at least in the case of Arifa Jan. When she applied for an industrial unit license, she was told it could not be given unless she had the right kind of machines. "One of those machines cost Rs 25 lakh," said Jan. "I was getting that part of the work outsourced. My total start-out budget was Rs 3 lakh. How could I buy a machine for Rs 25 lakh?"

She spotted the chief minister at a fair and approached him. "I told him that your people are not letting me start. He looked angry and then told his secretary, this license needs to be sent now! He told me, 'Don't worry this will not stop your work.' In two days, the license was delivered to me."

Abdullah says that the bureaucracy issue will not go away in a hurry. "It is a legacy I have inherited and I cannot suddenly fire thousands of people. But if it were left to me, I would immediately halve the number of state employees. Since I cannot do that, I have to bring many issues right into my office to hasten the process."

As he sat with Ratan Tata, Rahul Bajaj and Kumaramangalam Birla, Abdullah said his thoughts were about what he could do rather than about the investment of corporate bigwigs. "I do not believe that our problems will be solved by external money pouring in. Big companies come in because they see some loophole with which to make even more money and as soon as that goes, they exit. In the 1980s, HUL [Hindustan Lever] used to have a big factory in Jammu because the monopolies and restrictive trade practices law was not applicable in the state. The moment it was introduced, they packed up and left.

"So my focus is clear—entrepreneurs within the state. People who will definitely stay here," says the chief minister, who has been quoted as saying that enterprise cannot wait until "all the guns fall silent."

He needs to hasten the process of the state government's push into the support of indigenous industries, especially since the central government's thrust programs (such as Udaan and Himayat, which were launched in March 2012 to train 8,000 professionals for industries such as information technology and placement at companies like HCL, Wipro and TCS) are stuttering with only 139 students trained so far.

Haseeb Drabu says that instead of such programs, the state government needs to focus on a "quick double formula." "Look at it this way, in indigenous craftsmanship, for years, through all the troubles hundreds of thousands of people have continued in business. We calculated when I was at the J&K Bank that with a sustained push to provide finance to them, each crafts family which now employs two members can easily employ four—that's three or four hundred thousand jobs right away! And then spend money on marketing the goods—why has the price of a Kashmiri shawl remained stagnant more or less for more than 30 years now? There you have it—simple solutions that can immediately bring prosperity."

For the first time, says Gazzala Amin, sometimes called Kashmir's Queen of Lavender, there is a sense of urgency among many entrepreneurs and young people.

The 48-year-old started Fasiam, an aromatic plants and oil extraction business, with Rs 8 lakhs seven years ago. Today her cultivation is spread over 2,000 canals of land (20 canals = 1 hectare or 2.47 acres), and she exports quality lavender oil everywhere from Turkey to France and China. Amin points to the global flavors and fragrances market set to hit $26.5 billion by 2016 and says Kashmir can develop as an essential oils hotspot.

Lavender is prized for its linalool molecule, the perfume molecule that is used in cosmetics. The molecule contains esters that give it strength and purity, and Kashmiri lavender esters are often comparable to French lavender esters.

In her three hilltop farms at Sonawari, Pulwama and Tangmarg, Amin produces five crops a year, one ton each of lavender, *Rosa damascena* (damask rose), rose-scented geranium, clary sage and rosemary.

This is where she dreams of creating "an Indian Body Shop." "We have everything. Kashmir can grow some of the best quality aromatic plants in the world. We also have a lot of barren land where maize cannot be grown but aromatic plants can be grown there. This land can be used to get up to Rs 3 lakh per hectare," says Amin.

"There is so much opportunity that is being wasted."

Mudasir Mir says that's what he tells Omar Abdullah, who is also the power minister of the state, each time he meets him. In a power-deficit state, Mir's Magpie Hydel has three small hydro-power plants at Bandipur (10 MW), Tangmarg (10 MW) and Poonch (20 MW).

He says that, at the moment, Kashmir has "enormous pent-up entrepreneurial demand." "There can be 40–50 power plants in Kashmir in hydel power which is so much cleaner than coal but very little moves without the personal intervention of the chief minister. How many files can he personally move?"

The Fordham University MBA says entrepreneurs in Kashmir have decided to see that "the glass is less than half full." "Half full is where we realize that there is so much infrastructure missing in the state, and less than half full is where the bureaucracy and politics stifle things, but I think there is an overall sense that we must get things done in spite of all the problems.

"At least the guns are silent now."

◆ ◆ ◆

BUT EVEN WHEN THE GUNS WERE BLAZING, ONE KASHMIRI BANK KEPT the spirit of enterprise alive. In a sense the story of J&K Bank and its success is the story of how enterprise has been at the forefront of keeping hopes of peace alive in the valley.

Hear the tale of Ahjaz Ahmad, for instance. With the nonstop rattle of AK-47 gunfire and grenades going off right outside the door of his office at the Tourist Reception Centre in downtown Srinagar, Ahmad got a call from his boss, who told him to get out. The 45-year-old branch manager of J&K Bank refused. In the moment when he knew he might die, Ahjaz Ahmad couldn't help for a moment thinking of the files.

It was April 6, 2005, one day before the start of a major peace initiative between nuclear-armed rivals and neighbors India and

Pakistan. For the first time the two countries had agreed to start a bus service across the Line of Control, which divides the Kashmir Valley from Pakistan-occupied Kashmir and splits the northern borders of India and Pakistan. The neighbors have fought three wars over Kashmir.

A bus service would be a great step forward.

But around 4:00 p.m. the day before, when Ahmad heard the first gunshots, he knew that militants opposed to the peace initiative had struck. But he wouldn't leave. "The office was full of financial records. We couldn't have let it burn. These were records of us, people like me, the ordinary Kashmiri, our neighbors and friends."

So Ahmad and four other staff members remained inside the office as gunfire and bombing continued outside for one and a half hours, even after everyone from ten other offices in the building fled, even after the building was set on fire.

By the time they escaped their ground floor office with black plastic bags full of files and a drive full of data, after the firing stopped and the terrorists had been killed, most of the building was charred, and all ten other offices were either destroyed or nearly so. More than ten people were injured in the fire.

Eight years later, Ahmad says, "I was very scared, but at that time we were not so (technologically) centralized like today; if branch records were destroyed, rebuilding them would take a lot of time. My clients were not unknown people. They were my neighbors, people I knew, my father knew, his father knew—how could I let them down?"

Companies like to tell stories of being integrated in their communities. It makes them feel good about earning profits, and it doesn't look too bad in the annual report either. But few companies are actually part of the rubric of the societies they serve.

Ask anyone in Kashmir—from the elderly houseboat manager to the award-winning walnut-wood carver to the dynamic hydroelectric plant manager—and everyone will tell you that Kashmiris feel that they have a personal stake in the bank. And not just because the state of Jammu and Kashmir is a majority (53 percent) shareholder in the bank, making it the only bank owned by a state in India. All the other public banks are owned by the central government.

At a time when India's banking industry is in deep crisis and the gross non-performing assets (NPAs) of 40 listed banks went up by 43 percent in one year, J&K Bank had one of the lowest NPAs in Indian banking. Gross NPA for the end of March 2013 was 1.62 percent. Net NPA was only 0.14 percent, far lower than most of its industry peers that are roughly the same size, such as Allahabad Bank (3.19 percent), UCO Bank (3.17 percent), Punjab National Bank (2.35 percent), Indian Bank (2.26 percent) and Canara Bank (2.18 percent). India's largest banks, ICICI, Axis and State Bank India, also have higher net impaired loans of 0.77 percent, 0.32 percent and 2.10 percent. One of the reasons for the low NPA is captured in the data of the bank's advances, or lending. Until June 2013, 56 percent of advances were in agriculture if one looks at an all-India level. Outside the state this is a mammoth 83 percent. In the state, agriculture trails personal loans (32 percent) by 12 percent. Basically, J&K Bank does not lend to the kind of high-risk infrastructure and real estate projects that cause big holes in the balance sheets of most banks. It is one of the few banks that even managed to recover most of its money lent to the defunct airline Kingfisher. "We sold pledged shares as soon as the United Breweries and Diageo deal was announced and managed to recover back more than 90 percent of the 100 crores lent back," says Shafat Ahmad Banday, president (advances and asset planning) at the bank.

To understand the J&K Bank, which has grown from 280 branches to 777 branches and whose net profit rose from Rs 1.48

crores to more than Rs 1,100 crores between 1989 and 2014 (with deposits of more than Rs 69,000 crores for the year ending in March 2014), you need to understand its unique place in a troubled valley that has seen terrorist attacks from separatists for two decades in which around 50,000 people have died according to government statistics. And yet, during the decade of the worst militant attacks, between 1989 and 1999 (the year when India and Pakistan fought a war over Kashmir in the mountains of Kargil), the bank grew its net profit to Rs 85 crores from just over one crore as 67 new branches were added. It's an institution that grew rapidly during some of the most violent years in the Himalayan valley. It is an institution that veers between wanting to reach out into India, and even outside India, and wanting to retain monopoly business in the valley. As the main lender to most budding enterprises, it is perhaps the most vital cog in the green shoots of entrepreneurship that Kashmir has seen over the last one and a half years. It is perhaps the only bank in India that customers constantly refer to as "our bank." In Kashmiri business, J&K Bank is the only really big success story. It has no real state-owned competitor of similar size, and even the closest private businesses have a turnover of an average of only around a couple of hundred crores.

Analysts' reports endorse the bank's performance. "J&K Bank's credit growth is expected to outpace the industry while maintaining a (higher than competitors') NIM (net interest margin) of 4.1–4.3%. We maintain a 'buy' rating on the stock," says an ICICI Securities report.

J&K Bank's nearest national rivals, such as Canara Bank (deposits of around Rs 71,000 crores), have NIMs of around 2.3 percent.

Brokerage firm Anand Rathi in a recent report pointed to the fact that gross NPA of the bank grew 6.5 percent quarter on quarter with fresh slippage of only 1.2 percent of loans or "lower than that reported by most banks in 2QFY14," and with NPA coverage of 89.1 percent or "highest of its peers," the bank gets a "buy" rating. Says Vaibhav Agarwal, vice president, research (banking), of Angel Broking: "The stock is trading...at a higher end compared to peers, which factors in its better asset quality performance vis-à-vis peers even in a challenging macro environment."[4]

In a curious turn of events, if you look at the history of the bank, which started when Kashmir was still the princely state of Kashmir, the only Muslim majority state in British India with a Hindu ruler, it's possible that the militancy was the best thing that could have happened to the bank. (Though of course in troubled Kashmir no one quite puts it like that.)

Hari Singh, the ruler who dreamed up the bank in 1930 (it was finally started in 1938), wanted a financial institution of his own partly because his landlocked mountain state had little service from the big banks of the Raj—Punjab National Bank, Grindlays Bank and the Imperial Bank of India (the colonial avatar of the State Bank of India). The idea was to have a bank that was majority owned by the state of Kashmir with the rest of the equity with the people of the state.

The first shareholders of the bank included—apart from the government of Maharaja Hari Singh—the prime minister Gopala-Swami Ayyangar, the home minister, the revenue minister, a prominent merchant, and even a student.

Hari Singh was also the ruler who signed the famous instrument of accession to join his state with the union of independent India in 1947, though Pakistan has always claimed that as a Muslim majority region it ought to be with Pakistan. What this has meant for the bank is that it has—or at least had—always enjoyed unique privileges under Article 370, which gives special status to Jammu and Kashmir in the Indian constitution and in its own constitution. This means the state, at least on paper, has autonomy on many issues—though it is dependent on Indian money and security for almost everything. There are disputes about how this special provision works politically, but what it meant for J&K Bank was that, until 2011, it was the banker or "lender of last resort" to the state of Jammu and Kashmir. Other Indian states all bank with the central federal bank, the Reserve Bank of India (RBI). "Lender of last resort" is a term used for the bank that is the primary source of funds for any government. Because of the unique nature of political autonomy under Article 370, Jammu and Kashmir had its own banker, but in 2011 RBI took over this role as part of recent efforts by the Indian government to foster greater integration of the national financial system. Some of these efforts have been controversial, including the revival of a debate on whether Article 370 ought to exist.

"You can say we have a sort of old fashioned relationship with our customers," says Mushtaq Ahmad, chairman and CEO of the J&K Bank. He says the impact of our troubled times, the salary and pension accounts of all government workers and, until recently, being banker to the state has created a depth in relationship building, especially across the Kashmir Valley, that is very difficult for other banks to replicate. "We are a product of a unique combination of events."

There are numbers to back this depth claim. Of the 8,600,000 adult population of the state, 7,600,000 have accounts in J&K Bank. It has a branch in every single block (a district subdivision) of the state and is a near monopoly.

What this means is that Ahmad gets stopped often on the street. "I will be in a shop buying something and suddenly someone will come up and say, sorry to bother but I am stuck with this in this branch of yours, you have to help me. Almost everyone has my mobile number," says Ahmad, who says he often has to keep his mobile phone on silent; but everyone gets a call back from his office. He laughs that it doesn't make his wife happy.

Nazir Mir spent nearly 25 years taking loans of a few lakhs at a time from the bank until 2004, when, with his son Mudasir, he decided he wanted to be an electricity producer. "I was a construction and real estate man. My son had an MBA from America (Fordham University) but we had no experience in power, and yet power is what I had set my heart on," says Mir.

Between 2004 and 2005, the Mirs approached nearly every big bank in the valley—from Punjab National Bank to the State Bank of India—but everyone seemed skeptical. "We wanted to reach out to everyone to see what was the best deal we could get, but there was a lot of reluctance," says Nazir Mir. Some of this reluctance continues even today. To understand the reason, you have to understand where the Kashmir Valley stands today politically. It's a critical period for Kashmir. After an extended period of relative peace since the stone-pelting mass protests of 2010, the hanging of Afzal Guru (a Kashmiri accused of being part of the 2001 terror attack on the Indian Parliament, he was sentenced to death in 2002 and hung to death in 2013 after a final mercy plea was rejected by the Indian Parliament) marked the start of another sullen phase for the valley. A German embassy–supported concert by the renowned India-born conductor Zubin Mehta saw a security shutdown of Srinagar and four protestors shot dead in clashes with security forces.[5] In May 2013, the former RBI governor Duruvuri Subbarao complained about banks in Kashmir failing to lend more locally but after the concert—and with a revival of shelling between India and Pakistan across the border—Kashmir is in a state of unrest again, with protests flaring in many areas. Such is the fear of separatists taking advantage of the situation that India's biggest political parties, including Kashmir's ruling

Nationalist Conference, are asking the Election Commission and the courts not to extend a NOTA (None Of The Above) button, which was being unrolled in state polls in November 2013 and would be a feature in electronic voting machines in the national polls in 2014, to the Kashmir Valley. They fear that separatists will ensure waves of NOTA votes, which will be an indirect referendum on Indian control of Kashmir. (In fact, NOTA had little effect. In the national polls of 2014, barely 1 percent of voters used the NOTA option.)

So Mir says that then, as now, he prefers to "go to the bank that understands us best." "No one ever goes to the right counter in a J&K Bank branch"—because customers always know some people in the branch, maybe their relative, neighbor or acquaintance, and they walk right up to them. "This relationship is their power," says Mir, who now has loans of Rs 60 crores for his hydropower plants. It's the relationship almost every business owner of note in the valley has with J&K Bank. This year the bank's annual report celebrates this. Khwaja Saifuddin of Saifco, who is one of the most prominent builders in the valley and is also the owner of the Taj Vivanta Hotel? The bank has been lending to Saifco since 1955. SA Rawther Spices, one of the biggest spice exporters? First took a loan of Rs 20 lakh, now has borrowings of Rs 100 crores. India Builders, one of the biggest real estate companies? Exposure level has risen from Rs 11 crores to Rs 300 crores in 20 years.

To understand this, I went to meet J&K Bank vice president Viqar ul-Mulk Nazki, a man so famous in Srinagar that he even has a Facebook fan page called "Mr. Viqar ul-Mulk Nazki inspires me."

I met Nazki, a portly, ever-smiling Santa Claus of a man, in his Srinagar city center office with a bunch of his old clients. They were berating him for various things. "Nazki *saab* is very influential," says one man who builds bridges, "but he is not very pushy with the RBI. Why is the RBI not focusing enough on lending?"

Another who is a wholesaler of shawls complains that the bank should "give a big push to the government to build better infrastructure" in Srinagar. "J&K Bank should be involved in beautifying also," he says.

It is almost a monopoly business, one trader tells me, "maybe not absolutely accurately on paper but in the mind—and monopoly makes people lazy."

Through it all, Nazki barely says anything; he just smiles a lot and passes around a nonstop stream of chocolate biscuits and *kahwa*, the sweet, clear tea of Kashmir that is infused with saffron and diced almonds.

As the complaining comes to an end, someone gets a call on his mobile, and the group prepares to leave, but not before the bridge builder tells me, "Anyway, whatever it is, if anyone is putting money into any other bank in Kashmir, he is a bloody fool!"

When they are gone, Nazki guffaws. "You see, in an Indian family people are always fighting, no? It is like that here." But there is economic reasoning behind both their complaints and J&K Bank's slight complacency. It is because of these unusually strong community ties that the bank has such delightfully low NPAs. Those rock-bottom NPAs mean the bank can show an ever-rising provisioning coverage ratio (the amount of money it sets aside as coverage for bad debts to the total amount of nonperforming assets), which has risen from around 60 percent in 2009 to an all-time industry record-beating high of 94.01 percent this year. This naturally makes it a stock market favorite. The stock has risen 70 percent since 2011.

The fact is that other banks have never recovered, at least psychologically, from the militancy years. They take, but they are still not sure about lending it back.

What happened was that, basically, the Hindu Pandits were not the only ones who fled when terror came to Kashmir. Most other banks also shut down for two reasons—most of their staff was Hindu, and in many cases there were several staff members from outside Kashmir.

That is how J&K Bank became almost a monopoly in Kashmir. Even today, the wariness shows in the lending patterns of other banks. In the last five years, the bank's CDR, which measures how much money a bank is taking from depositors and how much it is lending back, has never dropped below 60 percent. The RBI comfort level is around 40 percent. One could argue that this is not just because of lending in Kashmir—after all, by its own admission and because of limited business lending opportunities in Kashmir, the bank collects more in Kashmir but lends more outside the state. It gets 64 percent of its deposits from Jammu and Kashmir but lends 39 percent in the state. Outside Kashmir, the numbers basically just reverse.

But here's the thing: J&K Bank's lending volumes on home ground outstrip all its competitors. Take a look at the first quarter of FY14: of the total credit of Rs 2,859.24 crores given out in the state, J&K Bank alone accounted for 67 percent, with all the remaining 39 banks put together giving out the rest.

One look at where the bank makes money explains the strategy. Even though it lends more outside the state, it gets 71 percent of its gross profits from this one state. The remaining 29 percent comes from business across India. That's because its net interest margins in Kashmir are 6.20 percent compared to 2.58 percent outside the state.

"Quite simply, we earn much more from the money deployed within the state than outside. It is far more expensive for us to try and earn from outside. The land here is much cheaper, labor costs are lower, NPAs are low—it makes perfect sense for us to keep diving deeper into this market," says Banday.

It is a depth that was built at the height of the militancy. In those years, bank employees would regularly open branches during curfews, personally deliver cash to the homes and offices of clients and even do foreign exchange deals from home and by telephone.

For instance, there was a time in 1990 when the valley shut down for three months in one of the longest strikes. Abdul Rauf, the HR head of the bank, says employees would get calls from customers who were waiting urgently. "Those were desperate times. Often there would be no paperwork since we couldn't go to the office. So we would go to a branch, open a side door, with someone else keeping check if anyone was watching, take out cash and rush out. We gave loans on word of mouth because we believed that this was not our money but the money of the people," says Rauf. "Those years have never been forgotten."

This continued even when people were hurt. In 1993, a cashier was shot as he was trying to transfer a client's cash to a branch. He delivered the cash to a nearby office of the bank before going to the hospital.

In 2005, a branch manager was kidnapped by militants. It turned out he knew someone among them, the cousin of a neighbor. They politely asked him to help out in releasing some stuck loans and let him go. The bank does not reveal names of people who directly came into contact with rebels even today because there's still a threat to their lives.

In all this, the bank also reached out to the most far-flung areas of the Kashmir Valley, like Zanskar or Dawar in the Gurais Valley, where there was often no all-weather road, often not even electricity. As of March 31, 2014, it had 777 branches, more than 80 percent of which are in Kashmir.

The current chairman, Mushtaq Ahmad, says that in the next five years he would like to see the business of the bank divided equally between inside and outside the state. As Ahmad likes to explain it, here's what happened to the bank strategically: most of the lending for the bank in total and the bank inside the state is in agriculture (and it is pushing much further in this sector). The new chairman now believes that in the long run it will lend to allied businesses outside the state—for instance, if agriculture is its strength, it is looking to lend outside to food-processing companies. The final strategy to be applied is tapping into the Kashmiri diaspora, so they are trying to see if they can open in Dubai and London and open more branches in India, including in Kerala, Karnataka, Gujarat and the city of Mumbai.

Some of this transformation began with Haseeb Drabu, who says that during his tenure as chairman of the bank from 2005 to 2010 he figured out a basic thing: Jammu and Kashmir had about 1 percent of the population, but contributed only 0.6 percent national GDP, 0.2 percent of personal credit and 0.12 percent of productive credit. The bank's CDR was around 31 percent.

"We went out to find entrepreneurs and give them credit," says Drabu, who focused on opening new branches and lending to small and medium-sized businesses in Kashmir. Advances between 2005 and 2010 grew from Rs 11,500 crores to more than Rs 23,000 crores. Net profit grew five times, from Rs 115 crores to Rs 512 crores. CDR rose to an all-time high of 62 percent.

One of the people who applauded this growth is 62-year-old award-winning carpenter Khalil Mohammad Kalwal. "People like me can only take small loans," says Kalwal, "and apart from J&K Bank, no one has ever really considered us safe bets." He has a current loan of Rs 26 lakhs.

This philosophy, started in Drabu's time, has now become one of the pillars of the bank—lending to more than 350,000 artisans and nearly 300,000 apple farmers. Lending to apple farmers alone has grown from Rs 100,000 crores to Rs 250,000 crores in the last three or four years.

But in August 2010, Drabu was abruptly fired. He got word that Chief Minister Omar Abdullah, with whom he thought he shared friendly terms, wanted him to resign. The word in the valley is that by bringing NPAs down to almost zero, Drabu had pushed corruption out of the bank.

At a time when the valley was in flames, with the army battling thousands of stone-pelting youth protesting the presence of the Indian Army in Kashmir and the killing of innocent Kashmiris who were then passed off as terrorists—what was beginning to be called the "new intifada" of Kashmir—the chief minister was put under enormous pressure. Some of the protests were politically motivated and a deal was offered, it is rumored, to Abdullah to stop the violence. A top bureaucrat told me, "The deal was let go of Drabu and the violence will stop. It was not the only criterion, but it was one of the important ones."

Ask Drabu whether he believes this is true, and he smiles. "The bank is a unique place. I have to say that Omar told me that he would not interfere in my working and through my entire period, he kept his word. Not once did he tell me what to do, even when I disagreed with him.

"But of course there are many vested interests at play and the chief minister is just one of them. There are many ways for pressure to be created." Chief Minister Omar Abdullah was not available for comment on Drabu's statements despite repeated efforts.

There might have been more to Drabu's story than this. A fervent proponent of Kashmir's autonomy, he was a fierce critic of RBI intervention in the state's banking and indeed was seen as one of the main hurdles to the switch in lender-of-last-resort status. In 2013, when the Securitization and Reconstruction of Financial Assets and Enforcement of Security Interest Act (SARFAESI) of 2002 was due to be applied in Jammu and Kashmir (pending judicial clearance) through a government ordinance, Drabu wrote in protest that this would further erode Kashmir's financial autonomy.

"I don't think banks from outside Kashmir really understand what is needed in the state," Drabu told me. "So this whole thing of them expanding is a little futile. They think in terms of loans on asset collateral. But what is the asset of the master wood carver? It is his hands. It is what is in his head. It requires a different risk-taking ability and analysis depending on social depth to do this kind of banking. So I never believed our autonomy should be given away."

The current chairman, Ahmad, is more subtle. He echoes Drabu to say that his work happens unfettered: "You might not believe me but there is no day to day interference from the government in the bank. When we grow businesses in Kashmir, of course, it has a political impact too."

But he adds that the bank needs new horizons. "Of course we will keep growing in the state, but if we don't also grow outside, it will restrict us in the future. Growth in Kashmir is not infinite," says Ahmad.

With business has come peace, or maybe it's the other way around, but one thing is certain—there is an unprecedented entrepreneurial wave in Kashmir. "There is definitely a peace dividend," says Mushtaq Ahmad, who is preparing to ensure that the bank remains the biggest beneficiary of that dividend.

As this book went to press, Kashmir suffered its worst floods in history, but it was heartening to see that its entrepreneurs led from the front in raising money and material for relief efforts.

CHAPTER 3

THE SOCIALIST MONEYLENDER

R amamurthy Thyagarajan never really got along with his father. He says this fact helped him build a billion-dollar group.

"There was duty, but not much love and affection. In India, the expectation is obedience, but you see, I have never been an obedient person."

Disobedience, says the 76-year-old, has helped him create one of India's largest and most diversified non-banking financial corporations. His Shriram Group manages assets of $14.11 billion and clocked in revenues of $2.5 billion in FY (financial year) 12 with profits of $355 million.

But had RT—as everyone calls him—listened to his father, Ramamurthy, he would have become an officer of the Indian Administrative Service (IAS). "Instead I chose to join the Statistical Institute of India because I always loved mathematics. Then I took a job in New India Insurance. I came from a family which had around 300 acres of land, there was agricultural wealth, and a son becoming an insurance man was not very prestigious. My father was not pleased and till the end he did not trust me with the family money. He thought I would waste it, give it away. In a sense he was right—I am a socialist."

A moneylender claiming to be socialist would be a laughable oxymoron, except that the Shriram Group has had more than 35 years of successful business in an industry that is plagued with graft in India. Among recent debacles, 60 people committed suicide after a public deposit scam of the Saradha Group[1] in Bengal caused a loss of around $4 billion; and the Securities and Exchanges Board of India asked the Sahara Group, one of India's biggest conglomerates, to refund more than Rs 24,000 crores (around $4 billion) due to illegalities in raising money by issuing bonds.

The nine financial companies in the Shriram Group gave exits to investments from 12 private equity (PE) funds from 2006 to 2013, with profits of $403 million.[2] Four of those occurred between September 2012 and May 2013 (a period described as one of the toughest in 20 years of doing business in the country by PE funds), including serial entrepreneur Ajay Piramal's $304 million purchase of TPG Capital's 9.9 percent stake in Shriram Transport Finance Company, India's largest moneylender to truckers. In the last decade, 16 PE funds have poured $675 million into Shriram Group companies, and many have had big-ticket exits. TPG earned seven times its investment, and in 2009 ChrysCapital got back a 12-fold return on investment when it sold its 17.26 percent investment in Shriram Transport Finance for around Rs 1,400 crores. Profits at Shriram Transport, the cash driver of the group, grew six times from Rs 107 crores in 2005 to Rs 612 crores in 2009 and then more than doubled to Rs 1,360 crores by the close of the financial year in March 2013. In fact Shriram Transport is one of the best-performing companies in Indian private equity in the last 15 years, right up there with telecom major Bharti, Axis Bank and biotech giant Biocon.

The group is also favored to win a banking license at some point in the future as India's banking industry slowly opens to new players. And in April 2013, almost as a bonus, RT was awarded the Padma Bhushan, one of India's highest civilian prizes.

If you talk to anyone within or outside Shriram who knows the company and the people who run it, the word "culture" pops up regularly. It is this culture that has kept Shriram afloat, unique and prospering.

After all, it was only about a decade ago that Shriram had its worst crisis. After India opened up its economy in 1991, tearing down 40 years of statist controls, there was a boom in non-banking financial companies (NBFCs). By the mid-1990s, India had more than 40,000 NBFCs, and the share of non-bank deposits in household sector savings in financial assets increased from 3.1 percent in 1980–1981 to 10.6 percent in 1995–1996.

By the end of 1996, though, one of the biggest NBFCs, the CRB Group of companies, collapsed. At its peak, the CRB Group had 133 subsidiaries raising money through public deposits, bonds and debentures and had raised Rs 900 crores between 1992 and 1995. By the end of 1996, its promoter Chain Roop Bhansali, the CRB of the group, was in prison. In 1997, a worried RBI issued guidelines for the stringent regulation of NBFCs. The Reserve Bank of India Act 1934 was amended in 1997, giving powers to the RBI to issue directions to companies and to their auditors, prohibit deposit acceptance and alienation of assets by companies and initiate action for the winding up of companies. The amendment also provided for compulsory registration with the RBI of all NBFCs, irrespective of their holding of public deposits, for commencing and carrying on the business of a non-banking financial company; minimum entry-point norms; maintenance of a portion of deposits in liquid assets; and creation of a reserve fund and the annual transfer to the fund of 20 percent of profit after tax but before dividend.

The new regulations shuttered many heavyweights in the industry, including 20th Century Finance, Alpic Finance, JVG Finance and others. For the Chennai-headquartered Shriram, the bombshell came when the RBI issued a press release in May 1998 warning investors against investing in fixed deposits of Shriram Investments, Shriram Transport Company and Shriram City Union Finance since none of the companies were rated by a credit-rating agency—one of the key new guidelines introduced in January that year.

It was a moment the leadership team at Shriram remembers very well. "We had deposits then of around Rs 700 crores. If there had been a run, we could have gotten wiped out," says Ramchandran Shridhar, managing director and CEO of Shriram Capital, who was then regional head of Shriram Transport Finance in Bombay. (Sridhar resigned a few months after this interview.) "There were people who advised us to shut shop for a few days and wait for things to calm down. But RT was having none of that."

Instead Thyagarajan asked every office to remain open. "He told us, 'We have spent 20 years being close to our customers. What do we have to fear? Let us see if people lose faith in us; open every office; return the money of anyone who asks,'" says Shridhar, who spent 28 years in the group. He had been spotted by Thyagarajan when he was working in the accounts department of the Krishna Gana Sabha, one of Chennai's best-known cultural organizations, which promotes Carnatic music; RT encouraged him to take the chartered accountant examination. "'If people think we are cheating them, they will exit.' Very few did. Our customers stayed invested with us. Where companies were shutting down, we emerged stronger."

There is a tinge of an urban legend to this story, and several senior management have their own takeaways from it. Akhila Srinivasan, managing director of the life insurance company, for instance, says it was one of the things that convinced her that the job was for life. "It is difficult to imagine the kind of fear and negativity that was in the market at that time. The panic was spreading. That RT remained firm and calm astonished me. Unless you have the inner strength of truth, you cannot be so calm when everything else around you is collapsing," says Srinivasan.

Umesh Revankar, head of Shriram Transport Finance, believes Thyagarajan could stand his ground because he knew that the regulator—and the ratings agencies—did not really understand his business.

"Our core business in transport then, and now, is giving loans on second-hand trucks. The people we service cannot afford new trucks and yet getting more to buy a used truck transforms their lives. But they are termed high risk and therefore we could not get good ratings for our business in those years and struggled to raise money from banks," says Revankar, whose business usually gets an AA or AA+ or stable rating these days. For most of the first 20 years of the Shriram Group's history, its main source of revenue was public deposits as it struggled to raise money from banks or through equity investments.

"But the flip side of that was that barely anyone was catering to these clients and we had dealt with them successfully for years. RT knew that there was no reason for these people to desert him."

Thyagarajan says his belief came from the way he had built his business. "If you simply look at my business history, you will see that first I started with truck finance, and I was clear that I was going to help the poorest in that category, so the focus was on used trucks; then came the chit fund [a community-driven savings plan that accepts savings at interest and provides loans for household and other expenses],[3] again expanding the product portfolio to the rural poor that we were already serving. The chit fund had thousands of agents and so to maximize their use and provide more products, we started public deposits and then insurance. There has never been any grand vision, all a natural progression.

"We knew the people we serviced, we knew they needed help and we were giving them a service that others were not and we had not cheated anyone. As far as the regulator is concerned—well, sometimes, the regulator wakes up and punishes the good horses that have not bolted the stable since they cannot do anything about the horses that have bolted!"

Shriram's turning point came soon afterward, in 1999, when in what was then a massive act of faith toward an NBFC, Citicorp, the non-banking finance arm of Citibank, partnered with Shriram to finance its truck-buying clients. A year later, Shriram Transport began securitizing its asset portfolio of old vehicles and sold assets worth Rs 100 crores to Citibank. This was followed by an even bigger shot in the arm when Citicorp picked up 14.9 percent in both Shriram Transport Finance and Shriram Investment (later merged into Shriram Transport Finance) in 2002.

During that period G. S. Sundararajan was managing director of Citibank's small- and medium-enterprises business. He was poached four years ago by Thyagarajan to become managing director of Shriram Capital. "What is the core idea in raising money? Trust. No one can guarantee that an investment will work, so the entire business is a gamble on trust. What Shriram did not have before the Citi tie-ups was the trust of big investors," says Sundararajan. "People were skeptical; the model seemed too different, too focused on high-risk clients. What we at Citi figured in those years was to look at it differently—that here was a company that had figured out a niche, a true bottom-of-the-pyramid approach, and had very deep linkages with the community they served."

Shriram had earned that trust, but often not in the way that is easy for markets to understand. The reason is in part the life of Thyagarajan himself. Until about five years ago, the man who built a Rs 60,000 crore empire lived in a 1,500-square-foot apartment. He has never traveled business or first class and has never owned a car. Even today he rides to his downtown Chennai office on Burkit Road in a Wagon R (one of the cheapest Maruti cars in the market) or with one of his colleagues. His wife recently bought a car for herself with her household savings—it's a Maruti Swift hatchback, barely a few thousand rupees more expensive than a Wagon R. He says his wife forced him to build a house—two floors, each of 1,500 square feet, one for the elderly couple and another for one of his two sons—because they had never owned a house. " 'We were getting old,' she said," says Thyagarajan, who has never carried a mobile phone. " 'We must have a roof over our heads.' I was against it. I used to ask her, 'What do you need a house for? As long as I am there, we are renting, and after me our Shriram people will take care of you.' But she insisted."

Most of his colleagues seem apologetic about every perceived extravagance. I met Shriram Capital chairman Arun Duggal, a Bank of America veteran, in his office in the Delhi city center of Connaught Place; it is a clean, functional place in a dusty building where the air conditioning is perhaps the most luxurious thing, but he seemed uncomfortable even with that. "Don't go by this office," was the first thing he told me. "This is not what Shriram is. We are far more modest. This I got because of my old habits from my banking days."

In Chennai, in another understated, though newly built office that looks more like a small, quiet middle-class apartment block than a corporate tower, Akhila Srinivasan echoed Duggal. "You should have come to our old office, very basic. That's Shriram. We don't like too much show."

The best example of this austerity is the Shriram "financial supermarket" in Chennai's broken-down Sorrento Building. In an office that looks like a sweaty, fly-infested graveyard for government files, regional manager S. Anandha Natarajan clocks business of Rs 15 crores a month, giving personal loans and gold loans, taking public deposits, and operating chit funds with a gaggle of ancient computers, a skeletal staff, and nine grime-encrusted inverters. The only air conditioning is in Natarajan's room. He explains the Shriram austerity best. "We were taught the moment we joined that the only way we could succeed is if we are close to the people who take money from us and give us money," says Natarajan, who has been with Shriram Chits since 1997. "But when such a person comes to our office and sees all fancy stuff, air conditioning everywhere, very Westernized, everyone in uniform, they are turned off, and we immediately put a distance, a barrier between them and us. How can we take money from them and yet have a lifestyle so different from them? The founder taught us that in order to truly serve the community, we must live their lives, like them."

Even the most ostentatious managers of Shriram agree it is a formula that works. Shridhar and a few others are the only top managers in Shriram who own luxury cars. He has a BMW in which he sometimes gives a lift to his founder, and he is looking to buy an Audi. "I like good cars. I like a good life and, to be honest, in my position, to push business I need business-class travel, maybe a club membership to meet the right people. Not everyone can be a socialist. We have to run business and sometimes do what that business needs," says Shridhar. "But RT's theory of keeping close to the customer has built this company. If it hadn't been for RT's setting an example, a huge part of the trust factor would be missing."

In my conversation with Thyagarajan, he seemed amused that Shridhar has a BMW and laughed indulgently and said he was not judgmental. "People should do what they like with their money. But as far as the business is concerned, who are we to say that it is all ours? It is as much the community's."

That's way T. S. Sivaramakrishnan, the secretary of the All India Chit Fund Association, says whenever there is a non-banking financial scam, he holds up Thyagarajan's example as a response. "Because Shriram Chits is the right example of how a chit fund should be managed and what a chit fund is. In India, any scandal happens—they call it a chit fund scam!" says Sivaramakrishnan, who runs his own chit fund, the Balussery Benefit Chit Fund. "In fact, most of the companies involved are not even chit funds and none of them are registered chit funds. All sorts of crooked Ponzi schemes are run in the name of chit funds."

A chit fund works with a pool of usually low-income depositors who are often not eligible for bank credit. Each member of the chit pool puts in a fixed sum of money every month for a fixed period of months. Usually the number of members and the number of months of the chit pool are equal. Every month, the members bid for the total pooled amount minus a standard discount. In the auction, the member bidding the lowest gets the amount bid and the remaining sum is distributed equally among the pool. At an average, chit funds that are regulated by state laws give a return of 12 percent to 14 percent.

Most scams in India like the Saradha fraud work not like a chit but like a Ponzi scheme that promises very high returns (Saradha promised 22 percent to 25 percent); the returns are financed by an ever-expanding number of depositors, and the money from new depositors is used to pay back older customers. As soon as the depositor pipeline dries up, the scheme collapses.

At Shriram Chits, usual interest rates vary in the range of 8 to 9 percent and could go up to 14 percent but only for senior citizens participating in chits for 60 months. "We do not offer get-rich-quick schemes," says Thyagarajan. "That is not our culture, that is not our business. Our business is to provide adequate finance to people in need. We like being conservative."

With more than 50,000 customers and assets of Rs 1,045 crores under management, Shriram Chits is a small but significant part of the Shriram empire today—like the venerable uncle in the family still capable of giving sagacious advice. One of its key strengths is that it can be held up as a rare clean company in a world bombarded with headlines screaming about chit fund scams. "Why were we never under political pressure? You will find the answer too simplistic but it's the truth—because I never wanted to get rich," says Thyagarajan. "Usually corruption in this happens when you go to ask for favors for either land or regulations or some diversion that will bring quick money. We have never cared and we have stayed under the radar. So no one bothered us."

Duggal says, "We would never give anything illegal and we want nothing in return—so I don't think there was ever any point of approaching us. We are just too conservative."

But that's not what you will hear talking to Shriram customers. Most of them say the reason they do business with the group is because it is not that conservative.

Narendra Salaskar, a 59-year-old trucker from Maharashtra, has bought and sold more than 40 trucks since 1987; each one has been purchased with a Shriram loan. "When I started, the banks didn't trust people like me to give money to buy one truck," says Salaskar. "Now that I own several trucks, I could today go to a bank where I would get 3 or 4 percent less interest, but it would take a month or 45 days to get the loan. It takes about 48 hours for me to get a loan in Shriram. In our business, the timing of the loan is key. If I don't get the money on time, I am not on the road. And every minute that I am not on the road, I lose money."

Even Shriram competitor Sundaram Finance has praise for what the company is able to do in vehicle finance. "Mr. Thyagarajan has run a campaign to bring down the time taken to sanction loans and in vehicle insurance claims that has forced everyone to bring down the time," says Srinivasa Acharya of Sundaram BNP Paribas Home Finance.

"People have been trying to emulate his depth in connecting with the low-income truck drivers to enter his business for a long time, but no one has succeeded in this the way he has," says Acharya, who worked in the vehicle finance business of Sundaram for 30 years before joining home finance.

Shriram Transport has a vehicle insurance turnaround time of about two weeks, lower by half than the industry average. Salaskar says one of the reasons he has stuck with Shriram is their turnaround time on insurance claims. With a net profit CAGR of more than 22 percent between 2009 and 2013, Shriram Transport is one of the biggest players in commercial vehicle finance and one of the most profitable with net profits of more than Rs 13,000 crores in 2013.

It's all a question of focus, explains Shriram truck finance head Revankar: "Everyone says they also do second-hand truck finance. The key word is 'also.' For us, it is not an afterthought. That is the core of our business. That is why we pay so much attention on how swiftly we can clear an insurance payout for a client. A second-hand truck breaks down more than a new one and that's why our customers who take loans for second-hand trucks need faster delivery of insurance claims."

Within the company, Thyagarajan has ensured loyalty in an innovative, simple way—he no longer owns the Shriram Group.

In 2006, Thyagarajan handed control to the Shriram Ownership Trust, where he and 14 other top managers have equal shares—a beneficial interest of 2.5 percent. The Ownership Trust also has 22 senior managers who get beneficial interest of 1 percent.

This is different from any stake or employee stock exchange. What this means is that the top 36 managers—at the level of a managing director or CEO—are entitled to money worth 2.5 percent (or 1 percent) of the value of the Shriram Group if they stay with the company until they are 60 years old, which is when they retire.

At that point, they get 20 percent of the 2.5 percent and the remaining 80 percent in equal sums every year for nine years. The 2.5 percent (or 1 percent) is based on the worth of the group when they hit 60 and does not vary as valuations do year on year.

In 2012, another trust, called the Shriram Enterprise Trust, was created with 25 percent equity transfer from the Ownership Trust to focus and invest in new enterprises. Six of the trustees are shared between the two trusts, and the Enterprise Trust has two additional members.

D. V. Ravi, managing director at Shriram Capital, says he knew that the wealth of the company would be divided equitably from the time he joined as a management trainee in 1992. "It is part of the process of entering Shriram; you get to know that if you work hard, the wealth is as much yours as the founder's. So while the trust creation only happened in 2006, we were all sure that it was going to happen for years. RT never left anyone in any doubt about this. The perpetual trust system is also our way of ensuring a perpetual leadership pipeline and a consensus-driven system."

How much was R. Thyagarajan worth when he voluntarily gave up control? He won't tell. "In my mind, I was worth nothing and my value went up to 2.5 percent," he says laughingly. This is not false modesty. Most of my two-hour process of trying to interview him was spent in his insisting roughly every 15 minutes that he didn't want me to write about his life but only about the company and its people. To dissuade me from focusing on him, he even said, "What if I give you wrong information and later on, in another interview, I tell a different story of my life? Who knows, it might happen. Best to avoid talking about me."

But I learned from Shriram insiders that the group was worth around Rs 20,000 crores in 2006 and the founder owned a one-third share. In one stroke that came down to 2.5 percent, and Thyagarajan became as much an owner of Shriram as many of his employees.

A rule was also created that none of the family members of the Ownership Trust would ever join any of the core financial services businesses. Even Thyagarajan's two sons have been allowed to work only in the nonfinancial arm of the Shriram Group.

Chairman Duggal says it is Thyagarajan's willingness to give up power and money that has built trust for the group. "It is difficult for analysts to figure the value of what RT has done," says Duggal. "If you look at the top management, any of them can get a job somewhere else and make more money but the sense of ownership is unique in Shriram." One top manager says at the managing director level, the salary at Shriram may be only around 30 to 40 percent of that paid by competitors, but people feel that this is their own company "for the simple reason that RT has clearly shown that he doesn't want to cling to power or ownership."

He also has nothing left to do, says Thyagarajan. "I have no ambition. I never did. I don't even today. The company will fulfill its own destiny and go where my colleagues take it." When pushed, he says he wants to start an institute dedicated to mathematics research, another devoted to the music of renowned maestro Lalgudi Jayaraman and a think tank to solve bureaucratic red tape. He is personally writing a simplified version of India's tax code. "But," he says, "it will be ridiculous if you write all this. You are really pushing me and that is why I am answering. Otherwise no one wants to know about me."

◆ ◆ ◆

RETICENCE IS A TRAIT THAT LENDER BINDU ANANTH SHARES WITH RT. The 37-year-old also hates wasting time, so she tries to get to airports at the last possible moment to board flights with minimum delay.

The only place where she is patient, she says, is her IFMR Trust. Six years ago, when she started the private trust (profits don't go to owners, or in this case, trustees, but are reinvested in the company), she had a novel idea. If Muhammad Yunus, the Nobel laureate microfinance expert, defined his model as "banker to the poor," Ananth positioned hers as "wealth manager to the poor."

Is there a distinction? Ananth thinks so—and on that idea she has gathered 445,000 borrowers across the states of Odisha, Uttarakhand and Tamil Nadu and in 2013 lent Rs 400 crores.

What differentiates Ananth from other microfinance lenders, many of who are much bigger than IFMR, is her philosophy. The heart of her lending model is intensive data gathering and analysis. The usual lender basically looks at some rough criteria, what Ananth calls "colour of credit cards-style" credit determination, or what your local bank would call KYC (Know Your Customer). The RBI defines KYC as a two-part process—identity and address.

Ananth says in her version of lending, to some of the poorest people in the country or to some with volatile income, like a farmer whose earnings might be concentrated in one part of the year (with the sale of crops) while there might not be much intake at other times, this kind of data is not quite enough.

"We seek to know almost everything about the customer. How many people are there in their family? What do those people do? What kind of assets do they have? What kind of lifestyle do they lead? What do they spend their money on? Who spends the most money in the household? At what periodicity is the money spent? The list is exhaustive. This data collection is the core of what we do," says Ananth. The data sheet also has the age and occupation of family members, a household balance sheet, including all assets (physical and financial) and liabilities (formal and informal), a household income and expenditure statement and goals for the household, including retirement.

The data is then fed into software that formulates a finance or "wealth" plan for the client. Ananth, an alumna of the Indian Institute of Rural Management and Harvard's Kennedy School of

Government, says her work is about training her field staff to sell a bouquet of services, not just give a loan. The idea is to look for clients who need services rather than for borrowers in a particular geographical area. The basis of most banking is geography. Banks target areas where they can tap into a large number of potential customers who have the ability to pay for their services and don't worry too much about the minority who cannot.

Microfinance institutions often do the reverse. Theirs is an access pitch, so to speak. They reach out to customers who are often very poor and live in very remote areas, and they charge high interest rates for this service.

IFMR's pitch is entirely different. The idea is to bring a branch to the clients and ensure that a client cannot only be given a loan but also sold insurance and pension schemes—whatever they need. The rate IFMR charges, around 12 percent, is roughly a third or at best half of what traditional microfinance lenders charge in India.

"The basis of most banking is geography, and we want to break that approach," says Ananth. "Our customers should feel that they are getting all the services through one representative who is a personification of a bank branch."

The finance scholar David Roodman,[4] a microfinance expert, has written that in Ananth's vision, IFMR is not a bank, a mutual fund or an insurance company, but acts as an "agent of all three." He calls it an "institutional platypus…a taxpaying not-for-profit."

Anil Singh Rawat is an IFMR client in a tiny village on the northern hills of Uttarkhand. He runs a roadside restaurant there, what is known as a *dhaba*. "There are very few banks here," he says, "and they take too much time to clear a loan. These people [IFMR sales representatives] sit and talk to us for a long time. I feel that they really want to know what I need."

In the early part of her career, Ananth worked with the Indian private banking giant ICICI Bank and was in many ways the protégé of Nachiket Mor, a former deputy managing director of the bank and chairman of its Foundation for Inclusive Growth. Mor was also the first chairman of IFMR and was instrumental in ICICI Bank's being one of the primary early investors in Ananth's ideas.

Ananth says sometimes she is accused of not growing fast enough, but that is exactly what she does not want to do—grow too swiftly and give up her core mission. "Banking is most empowering when it is a very specifically targeted service, but more often than not, that is exactly what it is not. It is formulaic and has a one-size-fits-all approach, which I think is the problem."

In her world, a client does not just need money; a client needs financial security that could sometimes come with a strategic life insurance or pension investment for recurring income.

It is a fascinating third approach to the duality of Indian finance—especially after the discrediting of the microfinance industry, including suicides in the state of Andhra Pradesh.

It is a mindset shift from, as Ananth recently wrote, a "buyer beware" model to a "seller be sure" model.[5] In a subtle way, she is shifting the onus onto herself and her organization to deliver the right package that is customized to the needs of her customers.

What makes Ananth's work fascinating is that usually such intricate customization, indeed even the term "wealth management," comes at the higher end of private banking. Bindu Ananth is taking that to the grassroots.

In their own way, both RT and Ananth are showing that lending to the poor can be a sustainable, socially useful and profitable business. Breaking many myths about the credit worthiness of the poor, their unique models are showing the way for financial inclusion in a country where the state could not, even if it wished to, ever provide monetary support to everyone who needs it.

CHAPTER 4

GUJARAT, RIOTS AND ECONOMICS

There was a time when it was Zafar Sareshwala's mission in life to get Narendra Modi arrested. Today there is perhaps no one among Indian Muslims who supports the former chief minister of the western state of Gujarat, and now, months after this piece was begun, the fifteenth prime minister of India, more emphatically than this scion of an old Ahmedabad business family. By his own count, he has "appeared hundreds of times in the press, both print and TV, clearing misconceptions about Modi." A quick Google search throws 10,400 results for Zafar Sareshwala—nearly all of them have him playing this debunking role.[1]

"I have always asked—what do you want? A better future or the idea of revenge, hate?" says Sareshwala, 50, owner of Parsoli Motors, the marquee BMW showroom in Ahmedabad, in addition to his family businesses in real estate and finance. "There is more to Modi than the riots."

This transformation has been neither simple nor swift (for Sareshwala it was taken a decade). But his change of heart is the biggest example of a slow change in perception driven by economics that was at the heart of Modi's campaign to become prime minister of India. This change in perception, which was kickstarted by Muslim entrepreneurs in many cases, finally resulted in Modi's Bharatiya Janata Party (BJP)—which won a historic victory in the 2014 elections—getting double the number of Muslim votes than it did in the 2009 election.[2]

Do all Muslim voters or entrepreneurs supporting Modi believe, as Sareshwala does, that Modi cannot be held solely responsible for the 2002 riots in which around 1,000 people—three-quarters Muslims and the rest Hindus—died?[3] Not quite. Some believe he could have done more. Some believe that he could have at least made a formal public apology, but they all have one thing in common—they believe that Modi is an agent of change, a man who can deliver growth and prosperity without favor or prejudice, and that his economic ideas will help everyone rise. That's why, for entrepreneurs, economics has been the most critical bridge between Narendra Modi and Muslims. And as India's economy slowed in the last few years, dropping to under 5 percent annual growth from a high of 9 percent, it made Modi's promise of jobs and a better life—literally encapsulated in his campaign slogan *acche din aane wale hain* (good days are coming)—resonate even among skeptics. Economics and the promise of enterprise won over many Muslims. The Centre of the Study of Developing Societies has noted that in states like Uttar Pradesh and Bihar, where Muslims account for nearly a fifth of the population, the BJP won an unprecedented 93 parliamentary seats out of 120.

There are many reasons for this—some that explain how Muslims inside Gujarat see Modi, which affects Muslims across the country. In Gujarat, 2013 marked the first decade in which the state's biggest city, Ahmedabad, had seen no incident of Hindu-Muslim violence. That was a first in a state that has a history of communal bloodletting (1969, 1982, 1986, 1987, 1990, 1992, 1998, 1999, 2002) since independence. That coincided with more and more Muslims voting for Modi. In 2012, Modi's hat-trick win in Gujarat saw around 31 percent of Muslims voting for the BJP. Different calculations by separate researchers show that in those elections, in areas where Muslims were either an absolute

majority or were most influential, the BJP won 8 of 12 such con-
stituencies according to one assessment, and 11 of 18 according
to another; this was in spite of the fact that in 2012, the Congress
Party won 61 seats in Gujarat, its highest tally since 1990. In the
2013 civic elections, where the BJP won 47 of 76 municipalities
(and the Congress Party won only nine with smaller parties like
the BSP [Bahujan Samaj Party] and NCP [Nationalist Congress
Party] winning more seats than the Congress Party), the BJP put
up 24 Muslim candidates and 3 Hindu ones in Muslim-dominated
Salaya in Jamnagar, a town in which 90 percent of the population is Muslim—and all 27 seats were swept by the party. Between
2009 and 2013 the BJP put up 297 Muslim candidates in various
elections in Gujarat, of which 142 won.

How did this come to pass? Not just through the peace dividend, though that was an important factor. Data shows that the
average Muslim has done well in Gujarat. According to the Sachar
Committee Report (2006), the most definitive report on the state of
Muslims in India commissioned by the (then) Congress-ruled central government, monthly per capita income of Muslims in rural
Gujarat was Rs 24 higher than that of rural Hindus. The average
urban income of Gujarati Muslims beat the all-India average by
Rs 71. The literacy rate among Muslims in the state was nearly
9 percent higher than the national average. Muslims account for
about 9.1 percent of the population in Gujarat but have bought
18 percent of the two-wheelers (an important marker for development) during the last decade; about 11 percent of the employees of the Gujarat government are Muslim, and 10.6 percent of
the state's police officers are Muslim. In fact, Gujarat has more
Muslims in police service compared to the percentage of Muslim
population than does any other state. Compare this to states like
Kerala, Assam and Bengal, some of the regions with the highest

Muslim populations. The Muslim population of Kerala is around 24.7 percent and Muslims account for 11.6 percent of the police force. Around 25.2 percent of Bengalis are Muslims but the number in the police is 8.4 percent, and Assam has a Muslim population of 30.9 percent with the police force being 21.5 Muslim.

What does this mean in the lives of ordinary Muslims? It means Gujarat has one of the lowest rates of poverty among Muslims in India. Only 7.7 percent of Gujarati Muslims are poor compared to more than 40 percent in Assam and nearly 24 percent in Bengal. Kerala is slightly behind at 8 percent. It is true that, as a state, Gujarat is more prosperous than Bengal or Assam and has more indigenous business enterprises than Kerala, but economists say that Modi has been able to ensure that during his tenure—and in spite of the feeling after the riots that he was deeply prejudiced against Muslims—the benefits of growth have reached Muslims.

The economist Surjit Bhalla has calculated that Muslims in Gujarat have had one of the highest declines in poverty anywhere in the country.[4] Gujarat has had the second highest relative decline in poverty among Muslims (Bengal had the highest decline, but its Muslims had a poverty level twice that of Gujarat).

"There is only one thing that drives Muslim support for Modi—good economics, and therefore better livelihoods and the promise of a better future," says Bhalla.

And so it is that many Muslims, especially entrepreneurs, but not confined to them, say that their feelings toward Modi's economics, if not toward the man himself, have altered significantly. Sareshwala's own story is illustrative.

I asked Sareshwala how this had happened while sitting in his all-white office at Parsoli Motors on the Sarkhej-Gandhinagar Highway in Ahmedabad.

He seemed slightly upset by the question. "What do you think I am? You think I am a fool? You think I am an idiot?" He isn't. His own business has been growing at 20 percent each year for at least the last five years. His BMW store sold nearly 600 BMW cars priced between Rs 30 lakh ($50,000) and Rs 1.5 crore ($252,000) in 2013—11 percent of these (double the number in 2012) were sold to Muslims.

The Sareshwalas have been in Ahmedabad for more than 250 years, working in real estate and finance. Zafar's father, Yunus, was a metallurgical engineer at the Indian Institute of Technology at Kharagpur in Bengal. On September 11, 2001, Zafar Saresh-wala was busy selling Sharia-compliant financial products across the United States and the United Kingdom. Between 1998 and 2005, when he was based in London, he used to work in the World Trade Center on trips to New York.

"But after 9/11, we saw with our own eyes how overnight everything changed. I just could not do business there anymore. The Islamophobia was too high—even people who had known me for years shied away," remembers Zafar Sareshwala.

Then came the riots of 2002, and "all that anger [of 9/11] was already inside me, and I thought, I have to do something." As in every previous riot, his family was involved in running relief camps after the bloodshed in Ahmedabad. One of their apartments, which Sareshwala's artist wife Asiya had bought, in Delight Apartments in downtown Ahmedabad had been burned down along with most of the building. The Shalimar Building, an office complex with 90 Muslim shops including a Parsoli office, had been gutted too. Shalimar is opposite the local office of the Vishwa Hindu Parishad (VHP), the orthodox Hindu nationalist group, some of whose members have been accused of fueling the 2002 riots. VHP leader Pravin Togadia has been questioned by the Special Investigation

Team looking into the riots about his role in instigating violence, but nothing concrete has been found against him.

"Everyone wanted to exit Shalimar and Delight but I was adamant. I did not want to sell. I wanted to send a message to Pravin Togadia that if you think that Muslims don't belong to this country, I want you to know that when you die, your ashes are washed away in the river and to the sea. But my bones will be buried in this land, as my ancestors before me. This is my land," says Sareshwala.

From that time, Sareshwala began campaigning against Modi in the UK, even attempting "as hard as I could to try and get the British government to deny him a visa and have him arrested for crimes against humanity in case he landed on British soil." He met Colin Powell, the US secretary of state and former army general, and appealed for a ban on Modi's entering the United States; he also filed a lawsuit against BJP veteran and former deputy prime minister Lal Krishna Advani.

Then on August 17, 2003, urged on by theater director and activist Mahesh Bhatt, Sareshwala and veteran UK-based Islamic scholar Maulana Esa Mansuri met Modi at St. James' Court Hotel in London during a visit by the chief minister. Sareshwala says Mansuri spoke to them for almost two hours, telling them that without justice, there can be no peace.

"Modi told us that his performance as chief minister would show the state how remorseful he was about the riots. He said 'judge my work, not my words,'" says Sareshwala. "I felt in that meeting that he was genuinely moved by what had happened and that he deserved a chance."

One of the biggest ways Sareshwala says he has understood that the chief minister means business is through his handling of five criminal cases in the last decade in which Sareshwala appealed to Modi. In each of the cases, there were Muslim men accused or convicted of grave crimes, including terror; one of the sections under which they were charged was 268, which declares a convict a public nuisance and therefore makes bail, parole or furlough (temporary leave from imprisonment on emergency) nearly impossible.

"But the chief minister has the powers to remove the convict from being held under Section 268 and in each case that I have forwarded to Modi on humanitarian grounds, he has removed Section 268 from it," says Sareshwala. The most defining among these was the help given to Habib Hawa and Anees Machiswala, convicted of involvement in the five 2002 post-riot bomb blasts in Ahmedabad that left dozens injured and came to be called the "tiffin bomb case" because bombs were packed in lunch boxes.

The family members of Hawa and Machiswala appealed to Sareshwala—one had elderly, ill parents, another a three-month-old daughter—telling him that without the removal of Section 268 from this case, it would be impossible for them to get any relief even to attend to family crises. It was removed. (The accused are now serving life imprisonment sentences given by the Gujarat High Court.)

Sareshwala would not directly confirm this to me, but almost every Muslim I spoke to in Ahmedabad told me that Sareshwala had become the man to approach for Muslims who were in trouble or who were seeking aid from the government. He has a "hot line" to Modi, I was told. What Sareshwala did confirm was that it was he who suggested to the chief minister that Arab envoys should be invited to Modi's flagship Vibrant Gujarat annual conclave in 2009. The Arab League sent a representative, as did Oman, Brunei and Abu Dhabi, some of the wealthiest Arab states. At that time Mahmood Madani, the leader of Jamiat Ulema-i-Hind, one of the largest clerical bodies, protested strongly. By 2013, he was agreeing with Sareshwala that there were more Muslims in prison in Maharashtra than in Gujarat and that Muslims were worse off in Rajasthan and Uttar Pradesh than in Gujarat. (This is not a unique volte-face but a signal of the times. In 2010, Ghulam Vastanvi, then vice chancellor of the Deoband Seminary, lost his post for praising the Gujarat development model. But in 2013 when another prominent Deoband cleric, Suhaib Qasmi, declared his support for the Modi for PM campaign, it barely created a stir.)

Sareshwala's role in all this has been to be the first to speak for Modi on Muslim issues. Mahesh Bhatt called Sareshwala after he received a message from Communist and theater activist Shabham Hashmi that Muslim slum dwellers had received no settlement after the redevelopment of the Sabarmati Riverfront in Ahmedabad. "I clarified that homes have been built for almost all slum dwellers, 68 percent of who are Muslims. Apart from a few cases stuck in court due to identification issues, everyone has got homes. You should go see them," Sareshwala told me.

"My point is simple—what do the Muslims want? The same as anybody else—we want a greater say in the affairs of this country. How will that come? Not by hiding in our ghettos but by becoming economically prosperous," says Sareshwala, and he lives by that example. His business worth is now Rs 200 crores (more than $33 million).

So I went to see the Sabarmati Riverfront development. The man who took me to one of the sites where the homes have been built at Vatva on the outskirts of Ahmedabad was Mushtaq Guliwala. A Muslim businessman, he runs a sari printing business called Honest Print Care. "One hundred percent of my customers are Hindu, most of my labor is Hindu, I can do nothing unless there is peace," says Guliwala, who says emphatically that he is no absolute Modi supporter. "I still believe that justice for 2002 has not been done—and any Muslim who tells you that they have moved on, well, I believe they are lying."

Although he is pleased that his business, worth about Rs 2 crores ($337,000) a year, is growing by 15 percent, he is angry that, in spite of numerous pleas, there is no proper road to his factory. "I am paying tax but getting poor service," says Guliwala. "I cannot say that Modi has changed or Modi has done great things for Muslims but yes, this much is true, as long as Modi is in power, no antisocial element can disturb business. You want to do business? No one will stop you under Modi."

When we reached the rows of brown concrete apartments for Sarbarmati slum dwellers in Vatva, Guliwala stared sadly at the patches of collected garbage here and there. "The houses have been built, yes, but it is still dirty. But then you know—dirt is something people themselves have to clean too."

To understand the conflicts in the mind of the Gujarati Muslims, you have to understand that Gujarati society is one of the most communally divided societies in the country. Such has been the proliferation of ghettos that some areas in Ahmedabad are referred to as the "border"—between Hindu and Muslim areas. But the Muslims have realized that the ghetto won't bring prosperity—and the community wants a share of the growth pie. At the moment Modi is the foremost Indian politician who is talking about fulfilling aspirations. Many are still skeptical about him—but there is no doubt about their eagerness for prosperity.

In a sense, the Muslim in Gujarat is coming out of the ghetto, says Kareem Lakhani, one of the most prominent Muslim chartered accounts in Ahmedabad. Since 1999, he and another Muslim partner, Armaan Ismaili, and the Hindu Narendra Tundiya have run a successful chartered accountancy firm—Lakhani, Ismaili, Tundiya & Co. Lakhani was once so poor that he sold milk to make a living and lived in a slum called Ram-Rahim Nagar. He says he supports Modi because "Modi has brought peace."

The three partners studied chartered accountancy together and then decided to start a firm. But in 2002, when the riots came, the mobs came looking for their office and the Muslim partners.

"Our office was saved because our Hindu neighbors gave them wrong directions and they couldn't find it," says Lakhani.

Today Lakhani's new office is in a building owned by Hindus, and most of his clients and staff are also Hindu. "When I was growing up, there was never a year when there was no tension between the Hindus and Muslims, but there has been peace for 10 years. Let me tell you why: riots are started and fueled by criminals, goons; ordinary people also participate, but the seed is always with criminals. Both Muslim and Hindu criminals are scared of Modi. No one talks about this but this is why he gets support—because the goons are scared of him," says Lakhani.

It is important to note that it is not the case that there has been no communal violence in Gujarat in the last decade; in 2013, the central government revealed the number of incidents (54) of communal violence for the first time—including 6 dead, three Hindus and three Muslims, by September of that year. The context is that these numbers were minuscule compared to 62 deaths in Uttar Pradesh in 2013 from nearly 500 incidents of Hindu-Muslim clashes. This sort of data has enabled Modi to retell his story of maintaining relative peace compared to a complete breakdown of law and order in Uttar Pradesh under chief minister Akhilesh Yadav and his father, Mulayam Singh (whose claim of being friendly to Muslims is so strong that he has been referred to as Maulana Mulayam because Maulana is an honorific used by Muslims for the pious) and their Samajwadi Party, which makes religious tolerance their core political plank.

"I believe that Muslims have to come out of their ghettos," says Lakhani. "I would say that 90 percent of Hindus are secular, and to curb violence you need strong law and order and that's why the demand for a strong leader is growing."

Lakhani says he realized that the tide was turning when he went to speak at a career fair at Juhapura, the most notorious Muslim ghetto in Ahmedabad since the 1970s, which was once called "mini-Pakistan." "Many of the speakers at the event were Hindu, and the response was very good. This would have been impossible for years," he says.

Earlier, Sareshwala had given me another example of changing times, also using Juhapura. "Even in Juhapura, there are now apartments for Rs 1 crore ($168,000) and Rs 2 crore; this is astounding for us who live in Gujarat and know its history," Sareshwala told me. What he is referring to is this: after 5,000 Muslims were killed in the worst riots ever in the history of Gujarat in 1969 and the state had nearly 200 days of curfew following the bloodbath, property prices in Ahmedabad stalled for nearly two decades. This was especially true for Juhapura, which is on the outskirts of the city. Ahmedabad was affected by the real estate boom across the country, and Juhapura too should have benefited, but in this city of "borders" that did not happen. Even with the real estate boom, had there not been peace and an anticipation of peace, the area in and near "mini-Pakistan" would have remained untouched by the boom.

To understand how Juhapura is changing, I went to meet Nadeem Jafri.

Until 2002, Jafri, a graduate of the Institute of Management Studies at Indore, worked as an account executive in the advertising agency Grey Worldwide in Ahmedabad. "Even though I had seen Hindus and Muslims in my neighborhood coming together and fighting the mobs, there was a lot of pressure from my friends and relatives to move to a Muslim majority place," says Jafri.

It was also the time when Jafri, who has a BS in physics and an MBA, decided to start a business. But he did not move to Juhapura until 2006 and clarifies that it had nothing to do with the riots. He says he held back moving right after the riots but finally saw the business opportunity. There was "also the family pressure to move to a safer location."

"I was already interested in retail and there was an opportunity. Juhapura did not have a large utilities and grocery store. People used to bring things from outside," says Jafri, who is from the Syed Shia Muslim community, who have close ties with the Chiliya Muslim sect. The Chiliya Muslims are famed restaurateurs and run most of the restaurants on the Bombay-Ahmedabad highway. So Jafri and seven partners pooled about Rs 60 lakhs in 2004 and opened Hearty Mart in the heart of Juhapura with contracts from many highway restaurants to supply wholesale groceries to them.

Today, with 12 franchise stores across Gujarat and a turnover of Rs 12 crores in 2013, Jafri's work has become a case study at the Indian Institute of Management, Ahmedabad (IIMA), where he has also lectured.

Jafri says he supports Modi's work—though he has reservations about the man—because it has brought development. "If we blame him for failing to stop the violence in 2002, we also have to give him credit for 10 years of peace," says Jafri, who once met Modi at a public event where they spoke briefly about growing Gujarat's economic potential.

He says all he wants is more development for Juhapura. "Already the locality is transforming. It has a series of new eateries where young people come for non-vegetarian [Gujarat is predominantly vegetarian] food," says Jafri, who has bought an apartment in one of the poshest projects adjoining Juhapura called Al Burooj, a set of apartment blocks complete with an air-conditioned gym and landscaped gardens that would not be out of place in the swish financial and industrial center of Gurgaon on the outskirts of the Indian capital, Delhi, which has mushrooming condominiums everywhere. He paid about Rs 54 lakhs ($91,000) for a two-bedroom home that is about to be delivered.

Standing inside Al Burooj, shaded by the palm trees that dot the neat walking track around the more than 300 apartments, Jafri said, "Does this look like a ghetto? No one actually wants to live in a ghetto."

♦ ♦ ♦

IT IS SEEING PEOPLE LIKE SARESHWALA AND JAFRI THAT MADE ALI HUSSAIN Momin, 32, decide to create Gujarat's first trade networking event of Muslim entrepreneurs. In 2014, 70 companies attended the event in Ahmedabad between February 7 and 9. The event was inaugurated by Modi in an unprecedented effort to reach out to the community.

Momin's Spider Communications, which does printing and public relations, and Muslim business networking platform Ummat hit a turnover of Rs 5 crores in 2013. His firm even got the hospitality business of Vibrant Gujarat, Modi's flagship annual business summit. "Many people told me that if you try and do a Muslim business event, you will face trouble," says Momin. "But the chief minister himself agreed to open it. He told me that every community needs to build since India desperately needs development and he was always ready to assist anyone who was building something. I have never faced any discrimination."

One of the people who had been a great source of support for Modi was the Syedna Mohammed Burhanuddin, the late absolute spiritual leader of the Bohra Muslim community—one of the most powerful business communities in India. The Syedna, who was born in Surat, had complete control over the Bohra community (though in later years there were some dissidents opposed to his absolute rule, which included payment to his office at almost every major occasion from birth to death). He gave many sermons around the world—several of these were in Gujarat—and inevitably he met Modi several times. They seemed to have developed genuine regard for each other. On the Syedna's death, Modi tweeted a condolence message—the first he had ever done for any Muslim leader.

The Syedna's control of his flock was complete until the end. When he died at the age of nearly 100 in January 2014, there was such a crush of his devotees that 18 people died in a stampede outside his home on Malabar Hill.

The Syedna ruled many, some say most, aspects of Bohra life—including, though never openly, who the wealthy business community would support politically with money and votes.

In Bombay, I spent a couple of days walking up and down the crowded Bhendi Bazaar and Nalli Bazaar lanes, the business center of the Bohra Muslims, asking traders about the late Syedna and Modi. It was two days before the 40-day anniversary of the Syedna Burhanuddin's death. Everyone I spoke to admitted that the Syedna's writ ran large in the close-knit community—and therefore he could impact the community's support of a politician, and in fact had, in the case of Narendra Modi. "The Syedna always told us that the Bohras had one principle—strengthen the hand of those who are coming to power," is all that Fakhruddin (who goes by one name), a partner at the glass traders' Fishfa Group, would say.

Farooq Umar at the hardware store Bellacasa is more forthcoming. "Can you tell me the name of the chief minister during the 1969 riots in Gujarat or 1992 riots in Mumbai [Bombay]? No one remembers. We need strong leadership."

Originally from Jamnagar in Gujarat, he visits the state every year. "Why should we not support Modi? Have you seen the electricity in Gujarat? It never goes. Have you seen the roads?"

From Bombay, I went to meet Fakhruddin Vanak, one of the most prominent Bohra Muslim entrepreneurs in Chennai. Vanak, 75, is chairman of Vanjax Sales, an industrial trolley and lift manufacturer. His Vanjax Sales had a turnover of Rs 22 crore in 2013 and grew by 10 percent. The entrance to his office has a large photograph of the Syedna.

Mention Modi to him, and the smiling man with twinkling eyes says, "Let me tell you a joke first. My granddaughter once told me that India was a banana republic. I was aghast. I asked her, who told you that? She said someone told her that Rajiv Gandhi used to say 'iss desh ko banana hai' (we need to build this country) and so, she didn't know Hindi so well, she thought it must be the same as a banana republic. I wonder if some people are thinking the same when Modi goes on about building the nation." He gives a little guffaw at his own joke.

Then he adds seriously, "We desperately need a sense of hope and growth in this country. We support Modi, of course we do. Naturally there was an impact in the community about Syedna's interactions with Modi. I hope that Modi will become prime minister and then fulfil all his promises."

Many Muslims—like their Hindu and other countrymen—await the fulfillment of those promises now that Modi is prime minister.

CHAPTER 5

IN THE COMPANY OF MAIDS

There was that time when Gauri Singh hired an employee. She seemed elderly but was probably younger, much younger, early middle age. A 40-year-old who could pass for 60. But in her line of work, Singh is often confused about the age of her employees.

Most of her employees are married at 13, mothers at 15.

"By the time they are 30, they are old women. By 40, they are broken. They are finished, they just cannot do hard physical labor anymore," Singh told me about the women of The Maids' Company.

After having worked for two or three days, Singh's new employee disappeared. About a week later, Singh learned that her body had been discovered. She had been found dead—robbed of the gold chain around her neck and her earrings, her sari hiked up above her legs, blouse torn and with blue marks around her neck. There was a strong suspicion of sexual violence. "She used to live in a particularly criminal slum and by the time I got to the police, they had already cremated her and closed the file," says Singh. "I stood in that police station horrified, and I screamed at the officer in charge. I told him that the criminals he was not stopping today—because the crimes were happening to the poor—one day they would attack someone richer. And then all hell would break loose for him." A few months later another employee, a 19-year-old trainee desperate for money, prostituted herself for Rs 7,500 ($126) to a local man in her area. That man led her to a gang rape by 17 men. She was thrown out of the van in the early morning hours in front of her home in the slum. The community shunned her, and she was left to bleed at the back of her aunt's house. A day after the incident Singh located her in her aunt's home, but before she could help the girl, in the family's panic to hide from the social shame, they sent the girl off to the village without medical attention. Soon, Singh heard that the girl was dead.

This time, the officer listened to her patiently and then gave her some advice. " 'Madam,' he told me," Singh remembers, " 'what kind of business are you doing? This is very dangerous for you. Next we will be coming to meet you in jail.' I didn't know what to say."

The Maids' Company employs some of the poorest women in India, an invisible workforce from all over, in the town of Gurgaon. A satellite city of the Indian capital, its groundwater tables are hitting crisis levels even as new Jacuzzi-sporting penthouses relentlessly rise to the sky These women are trained by Singh—who studied social policy and development at the London School of Economics—and her partner, Indu Bagri, and their managers in domestic work. Cooking, cleaning, washing, taking care of children—the all-women company provides all these services for a price. They are a new and unprecedented link between the two faces of India, perpetually in contact but increasingly distant. It is a complex, delicate, even dangerous balance that Singh negotiates. To glimpse inside her business is to comprehend India's many layers, static and kinetic, those ever-darting flickers of aspiration and of social ascendancy.

I have a job where I meet entrepreneurs every day, but Singh is different from anyone I have ever met—as is her business, which some people mistake for an agency that places maids. To understand what she does and why it is important, you have to understand the origins of both Gurgaon and Gauri Singh herself. Gurgaon is the schizophrenic, dystopian soul of India—a place where everything has gone wrong and right all at the same time.

The town is also called Millennium City because it sort of combined together many villages and emerged as a city at the turn of the millennium in the state of Haryana, which borders the Indian capital, Delhi. The melting was uneven—many villages remained—and Gurgaon, it seems sometimes, lives in both the twenty-first and twentieth century at the same time.

So Gurgaon has evolved only over the last decade or so into what it is today. Before that it was Gurr-ga-wahn, as the villagers call it, in their gruff Haryanvi. "*Gaon*" in Hindi means "village," and it was many villages then.

When I first used to go to Gurgaon in 1998 and 1999, the wide road that led to Delhi wound through a desolate, dry scrubland of emptiness, interspersed with a few pubs named after their respective milestones. A famous one was 32nd Milestone. The names accurately implied the sense of desolation beyond.

The ancient Aravalli mountain range spreads over Gurgaon. The mountains are Delhi's natural barrier from the yawning mouth of the Thar Desert just a few hundred miles away in the state of Rajasthan. From Gurgaon to the desert in Rajasthan is less than 500 miles, a drive of barely 12 hours, with a little help from the weather and traffic gods.

The Aravallis stop the sands from spreading. But not the city. Gurgaon is an altogether different beast from Delhi. It is as tall as the capital is low, as if to compensate for history, representing the tall tales it has had to tell itself about itself.

I watched this town rise—not slowly, not in hiccups of clumsy brick and tar, but all at once, a prefabricated hothouse, its dreams neatly brought in parts and assembled in a whoosh.

So it is a town of many tall towers in the middle of many small villages. We wanted so much for it to be our showcase to the world, the capitalist paradise after our years of socialism.

But we managed only a half-hearted, sometimes half-witted, version of capitalism. Gurgaon has let its people down. It is a town of refugees. Delhi was rebuilt at independence from the British Raj in 1947 by refugees from ostracism, by people who had lost everything during the partition of India and Pakistan, which saw the deaths of a million people.

Gurgaon's refugees were different. They came from across India, a large number from Bengal in the east and Uttar Pradesh in the north, and they searched for glass facades, plastic tags on smart suits, a lifestyle of high-performing corporate climbing and empowering anonymity. Gurgaon built itself in the image of its own aspiration.

But only after building the high-rises did they realize they had forgotten to lay sewage lines in many places, or to put up traffic lights. There was imported liquor everywhere, but almost no bus service.

A decade later, Gurgaon is still growing, the promise of penthouses still holding strong. But to paraphrase a Leonard Cohen song, there is a crack in Gurgaon and its makeup, a crack in everything. That's how the light is getting in.

The residents in their tall towers in Gurgaon have made sanctuaries of guarded peace amid the melee. Their remove keeps them secure against the public chaos. But they don't have the easy access to domestic help that they had in their previous homes, where they would ask neighbors about their maids. They would stand on the balcony and beckon maids going to other apartments. Ask them where they were from. Ask their names, where they lived, if they could come do the dishes every morning.

But no maids pass by anymore. They could not if they wanted to. The apartments have three layers of security checks around their manicured gardens. They are beautiful but secluded. No entry without verification.

So these days, many maids come from agencies. But most are crooked fly-by-night operators who exploit both the clients and the workers. In a worst-case scenario, some agencies run modern-day slave labor operations: the salary is paid by the client to the agencies and is held back for months or only paid in parts to the workers to keep them in perpetual bondage to the agent.

Hiring maids used to be all about unverified, even unverifiable, reaching out, talking to your neighbors, trusting their judgment. But while sullen, shiny Gurgaon is an ever-expanding city—its population grew in the decade between 2001 and 2011 from 1 to 1.6 million—it is not a trusting city.

This town of villages is also full of ex-villagers who are now flush with cash after the sale of their lands to real estate developers, but whose medieval lifestyles are at odds with the credit card–fueled modernity in which everything can be priced and purchased. Their sense of value has for centuries been determined differently.

Gauri Singh, who loves to motorcycle and sometimes gets impatient with Gurgaon's errant SUV-laden traffic, says she is sometimes afraid to give a speeding driver an earful. He just might pull out a gun. In this universe full of unlicensed, illegally purchased guns, an angry young woman behind a wheel—especially one in a car smaller than theirs—is the ultimate assault on the ego.

Singh wants to change all that. From 2003 to 2007, she worked at the Self-Employed Women's Association (SEWA), one of the biggest not-for-profit women's self-help groups in India, which brings economic security, jobs and livelihood to the most vulnerable.

It is a curious choice because Singh herself stands at the nexus of these colliding worlds. She comes from a wealthy family in

Punjab. Her late father was a prominent, socially well-connected architect. Her mother too is a celebrated architect, and her brother, a structural engineer, runs a successful real estate company that, among other things, builds luxury resorts in Southeast Asia. Singh's first degree was in architecture. She spent some time in the family business. But once she learned how to organize the poor at SEWA, it became clear that this was her calling. "I first thought of doing this as a not-for-profit. But then my entire strategy would be donation- and grant-based. I would never be able to create any assets or ownership for those who work with me," says Singh.

"To me the idea that the women who work with me, most of them barely literate, own a part of this company is a very powerful one," says Singh. The Maids' Company has 20 percent of its equity in a reserved pool that is owned by a cooperative trust of the workers. It has 200 employees, an equal number of clients and a turnover of Rs 1 crore ($168,000) in 2012–2013. Besides the equity, what sets The Maids' Company apart from placement agencies or the fly-by-night operators is the basket of employee welfare services that have been designed specifically for an all-women workforce. The equity supports these services. The employee welfare basket contains the following services: for cases of domestic violence the company provides a halfway house, a counselor for both the worker and her husband, and a link with the women's police cell; for daily sustenance, interest-free loans, bank accounts and linkage to insurance; for health security, home visits by a nurse, a 50 percent subsidy for all OPD (outpatient) costs and an interest-free health loan for inpatient expenses. These services address the issues faced by urban poor women, thereby ensuring a steady work force.

During her work at SEWA, especially while working with women at construction sites, Singh observed that domestic work was one of the safest environments in which women from poor backgrounds could earn money. It was where some of the poorest women—and some of the most desperate women—were engaged. More and more women in the low-income segment in urban areas were choosing domestic work, citing the flexibility of hours as the main reason.

Women from low-income backgrounds typically find work at only a few places in India. The young, able-bodied but very poor work on construction sites as human carriers—they usually don't get any skilled labor.

Women who have some education, especially if they are able to comprehend—even better speak—a smattering of English, get "indoor jobs," for instance as assistants at a mall where they can stay indoors in an air-conditioned environment.

But the women Singh works with are at the bottom of the food chain. They are sometimes not young enough to sustain long stretches of heavy labor on a construction site, nor do they have the skills for better-paying indoor work. They also often have children and cannot do eight- or ten-hour shifts.

"Working in homes is the best solution for the poorest women until they can upgrade their skills and move on. They can choose to work for four hours or six hours. The work is easy to learn and it is far more sheltered than a construction site or a mall," says Singh.

"But I also figured that I could only do this if I completely reinvented what domestic service really meant. For one—we provide a service. We don't provide labor." Most Indians, even in the wealthiest pockets, tend to think of domestic laborers as "servants" or as people with no really fixed terms of service or standardized pay. This does not mean that conditions for domestic work in India have not improved steadily and incessantly over the years, but terms and conditions remain fluid. Singh is trying to change that by offering "packages" of work hours during which domestic help is provided—four, six, eight or ten hours at different price points. The company does not provide help that lives with the client family and is therefore available 24/7, which is what many clients who pay the highest wages have traditionally demanded. The Maids' Company also insists on a compulsory one weekend day a week off, another traditional sore point. But Singh argues that this is the core of her value proposition—service, not servants.

Singh has had occasion to constantly reaffirm that in the past three years. Like the time when her office got a call from a client, a well-to-do apparently suave businessman who told her that he would take the maid to the roof, throw her down, pick up her body, and throw her down again—because she had been rude to him.

Terrified, the customer service representative called Singh. "Here's the thing—and this is one of my biggest insights—the moment I got onto the call, the client's tone changed. I have seen this again and again and again," Singh told me, sitting at her office beside a desk that had a sheet of paper attached to it. It was like an office homily. It said, "We must not hate people who have done wrong to us. For as soon as we begin to hate them, we become just like them, pathetic, bitter and untrue."

"As soon as I started speaking in English—the tone, nuance, verve, everything of the conversation changed. Suddenly the client was polite." But the company still decided to terminate services immediately even though the client offered a written assurance of the safety of the maid and an apology. Another time a client who worked at the United Nations threatened to have the client-servicing executive of The Maids' Company beaten up and thrown out of the complex for a minor incident. Yet another time, when a maid forgot to put cling film on some food, a client raised her hand and threatened to beat her.

In every case, especially if violence has been threatened, The Maids' Company immediately terminates service. Says Singh, "But the clients don't want that. They are accustomed to talking in a certain way to domestic help, and it is a mindset change, a jump in behavior for them to fix that. In their gated communities, getting reliable service is very difficult. When they recruit an agency, they do police checks but there is no guarantee that the agency would be available if something goes wrong, no guarantee that they won't disappear after taking the advance. We are available all the time." Most urban police in India advise the people to get a police registration of all their domestic help, like drivers, cooks and maids.

But sometimes things still go wrong. Like the time when a client accused the maid for stealing a chocolate worth Rs 2. This was in response to the client's first reprimanding the maid for being ten minutes late. The maid rightly informed the client that she would try to make it on time, but due to traffic, a delay of 15 minutes was sometimes out of her control. The client was upset that the maid answered back and took the issue to the company. The company repeated the maid's answer. This made the client angry, and to put the company on the back foot, she accused the maid of stealing a Rs 2 piece of chocolate.

"We, as per our process, immediately replaced the maid. Then the client came back to us saying they didn't care about the theft and wanted to continue with this maid," Singh says. There is, as she often thinks, never a dull day in this job.

India's 1.2 billion population means there has been no dearth of domestic help—even now mostly referred to as servants—for centuries. But, in a nearly unnoticed change, the supply is drying up.

Two decades of economic growth, though in fits and starts, have moved millions out of poverty. And two things are increasingly happening in India's biggest cities. The local supply of domestic labor, the "known" labor force as it were, people who, like their employers, have lived in the same area for years, is thinning. As residents of urban areas, they too benefit from the economic process—today's domestic help becomes tomorrow's secretary or clerk, gets a scholarship and becomes whatever they want. Economics has set millions off on a different path of social mobility.

The labor pool in the past did not necessarily need elaborate background checks and police verifications—at least I do not recall, and neither does anyone else I know, any such system ever being applied by an earlier generation. My parents certainly never got their help registered.

The second is what the Harvard philosopher Michael Sandel talks about when he examines the impact of the social exclusion between classes in his lecture "What Money Can't Buy: The Moral Limits of Markets" and how it never existed in the past.[1] I know what he is talking about. We didn't grow up with that kind of exclusion during my childhood in Calcutta. We grew up in a world of a sense of shared space and constant interaction between us and those who worked for us. We were not rich, not at all. We would have been what are now called the lower middle class.

Our help was poorer, but we shared many things with them. We traveled in the same buses. We did not have a car, nor did they. Their children played with us. Our playgrounds were the same. And once in them, the best child won—and they were often the best players, tougher than us, more willing to take a fall to stop a ball. At festivals like Holi and Diwali we often, though not each time, celebrated together with colors and firecrackers.

But that is almost absent in Indian cities these days. My niece, in her four years, has barely interacted with anyone but her own class and people wealthier than her. Yet ever-soaring reports of violence and sexual abuse mean that, when she was three years old, she was taught at her playschool to "tell Mummy if anyone touched your bottom."

This is the world of Singh's clients. Their social mobility has taken them, literally, off the ground. In their tall towers, they hunt for the solace of reliable service at home, but they have no access to it where they live.

Social mobility has also taken many of the old labor pool away—the "servants." They are being replaced by a new workforce that has just moved from the village and is unsure how to engage with the anonymous language of urbanism. Their existence in the eyes of the clients, and sometimes in reality, is unsettled and unsettling.

Hence the background checks, the police registration, the fear.

R. V. Anuradha is a trade and climate change lawyer who has been paying around Rs 20,000 a month for the past year for the services of two employees of The Maids' Company—one for twelve hours a day and another for six.

Anuradha lives in South City I, one of the first complexes built in Gurgaon. She says she could potentially get domestic help a wee bit cheaper, but "this service really relaxes my mind." "If the maid is going to be even a few minutes late, I get an SMS on my mobile. The rules are well laid out—one day of holiday, a Saturday or a Sunday every week. And apart from that, if my regular maid is absent any day, I immediately get a replacement," says Anuradha, a partner at the law firm Clarus Law Associates.

What is happening is a complete renegotiation of the social contract of domestic labor. Anuradha cannot—unlike my mother in the old days—ask the cook to help out with the ironing from time to time or to water the plants. But on the flip side, she has no reason to feel obliged to pay for the schooling of the maid's children—as my mother used to.

Singh calls it the mental shift from "servant to service."

Anuradha agrees. "It is a gradual process. Some of my neighbors still ask me why do you have to pay service tax for hiring servants? But it is a professional service—it is trained, all the verifications are done, and there is always a replacement. None of that is my headache—so there is a cost to that."

Around this pitch of convenience, Singh has built a business plan. "We realized that people would be willing to pay if the quality is really good. But for good-quality people to stay, the pay has to be good but that's not enough. We have to give them an opportunity to straighten their spine."

This is curious phraseology but curiously accurate. In the hierarchy of Indian class, subservience is often as much a physical manifestation as a cerebral attitude. Like the Japanese, Indian courtesy requires a small bend at the shoulders with folded palms to make an *A* in front of the chest.

A bent spine personifies deference.

But this supplication takes new forms of servitude as we go down the class ladder. Singh's employees, almost all of them, are regularly beaten by their husbands at home. They often arrive with cigarette burns on their arms, or a black eye, or bruises everywhere. Singh employs a nurse full-time.

Sometimes in the middle of the night, when they have been beaten and then thrown out of their homes, maids come and stay overnight in two rooms on the top of the office. They stay for a day, maybe two. Then they go back, to the same husbands, the same homes. I asked Singh why her employees don't leave their husbands, and she said, "Because then they have no protection. I don't condone this. It is a very complicated reality in which these women make tough choices. And their rational for this choice is 'What one man is doing, rape and physical abuse, every man will try to do.' In their world, without a man, a woman becomes public property with no defense. I am just repeating what reason the maids give to stay with their abusive husbands. We give the employee a basket of services, which helps support them through these tough realities."

To reach the office of The Maids' Company you have to cross the border dividing Delhi and the state of Haryana and travel for about five kilometers until you come to the Galleria Market. With its single-storied shops in a rough oval around a fountain, the Galleria is known as Gurgaon's Khan Market. Khan Market is the most expensive market in Delhi. Khan Market, once a quiet bookstore-filled neighborhood frequented by politicians, diplomats and bureaucrats who were lucky to get government accommodation in tony, tree-lined central Delhi, has now become a bursting, overpriced bazaar. But it still retains some pride-of-place clout—it is the only such market in the heart of the colonial capital that was built by British architect Edwin Lutyens in the early twentieth century.

In the constant competition between the two cities, things in Gurgaon are often referred to as "Gurgaon's this" or "Gurgaon's that." The Galleria Market is one of the nerve centers of Gurgaon. Two giant, swish apartment blocks lie beside it—Hamilton Court and Regency Heights.

The lane opposite the Galleria slips between row houses and a few shops, and the second left leads to a quiet three-storied house with one wall painted pink. The road outside is slightly broken but the paper banners on the walls and the garlands of flowers on the door make the office of The Maids' Company festive.

Singh sits on the second floor in a small sun-swept office behind a chipped wooden desk with a well-worn swivel chair behind it. A couch fills the other side of the room. I asked Singh if she keeps it deliberately understated. "I wish it were," she smiled, "I just can't afford any better."

In 2013 her turnover touched one crore rupees ($168,000), still small but the impact on her 200 employees has been enormous.

The first time I went to the office of The Maids' Company, I sat in the accountant's room beside Singh's room to talk to her employees. Lakshmi Bala Das does not live with her husband. She is 45, maybe 50. She is not sure. She is from the Nadia district of the eastern state of Bengal.

Her husband, she said, does not do anything. He has been ill for a long time. There is something wrong in his stomach, something also in his legs. He used to work in the fields, but now he just sits around in their village hut in Nadia. Das earns Rs 8,500 a month in Gurgaon. She has two sons. One of the sons lives in Delhi, another in Gurgaon. Both of them are married.

Das lives with the younger son and his wife. The children don't give her any money. "I give my younger son one thousand rupees every month. When they fight, my younger son and his wife, I leave the house and come to The Maids' Company office. I can stay here for a day or two until the fight calms down. And every time I visit my older son, I give him some money."

Up to this point, Das and I were having a fairly easy banter. I was asking, she was answering, it was moving along deceptively easily. Now she stopped. She was so silent that I hesitated to immediately spring another question.

Then Das said she also sends her husband money each month—though she wouldn't tell me how much. "He has bought a mobile phone with the money I send. He calls me every day but he does not ask when I will go back to Nadia—he knows if I don't send money, he will not get food to eat."

And just like that, the spine seemed to straighten slightly.

Singh's partner in the business is Indu Bagri. She is 41 years old and has been a social worker all her life. She is from Udaipur in Rajasthan. Bagri is Singh's alter ego; she is quieter then Singh and is the sort of person who exudes a sense of warmth but also complete control. Bagri also speaks fluent Hindi, an invaluable grassroots skill. Singh is less fluent, even though Hindi is her second language. Singh also speaks Punjabi, which is the language of her parents. Singh and Bagri met when Singh was working at SEWA. Bagri "organizes" the supply of manpower on which The Maids' Company is built and heads the women's cooperative. When they arrived in Gurgaon from Ludhiana in Punjab, Bagri had never been to the place, and Singh had never worked there. Bagri went from slum to slum, gathering women around her, winning their trust, dealing sternly with their husbands, especially if they were drunk, and talking to them about a different kind of domestic service. Service, not servant. "I am able to talk to them easily and freely because I never judge and I never assume anything," says Bagri with a smile. These are lessons her own life has taught her. Bagri's human-rights lawyer husband travels very frequently across Rajasthan and needs to be away for long stretches, so the couple lead independent lives, something unheard of in their sort of traditional village backgrounds. He was the one who was in the nonprofit sector and encouraged Bagri to work even though he comes for a very conservative family where the women veil themselves from the men. Bagri was the first woman in her own and her husband's family to work and has broken a lot of stereotypes of the classic Hindi-speaking Indian woman.

When, after just a couple of months, the first 200 employees of The Maids' Company suddenly failed to turn up at work, it was Bagri who went hunting for new recruits and negotiated with some of the old ones. What had happened was that the first clients had offered each of the maids a couple hundred rupees more, and they all quit en masse. "I had to explain to each of them what they really get if they work with us. Respect is a tough thing to explain to those who have never had any," says Bagri wryly. Within a month, the office had filled up with staff again.

All this helps Bagri understand women like Soni Parveen, all of 20 years old. Parveen was a Hindu Brahmin, the highest caste among Hindus, until she fell in love and ran away with her father's Muslim tenant. Her father was a shopkeeper and had given his daughter that rare thing—an education through Class 10 (10th grade).

But the daughter ran away and converted to Islam to marry her lover. These days he works at odd jobs—and beats her frequently. But Parveen, who has a radiant smile, refuses to leave him. And each month she dutifully puts her salary of Rs 10,000 in her husband Salim Khan's hand. Her parents, she says, are not sure exactly where she is, though she sometimes talks to them on the phone.

I ask Parveen why she does not leave her husband—and why she gives him her salary. "He respects me. I bring in money," she says simply. "Without money there is no respect."

Later Singh explains, "Without the money, there would be much more beating and maybe he would even have left her. Where would she go then? It would be much worse for her." She says that she doesn't condone this. "This is again a tough choice made in a complicated reality. We can only offer support in various forms so they see another choice but beyond that we can't change their choice. I hope that with a few years of economic empowerment they will start to make a different choice."

Singh says all kinds of nuances she could never fathom are now immediately apparent to her. Consider this almost Malcolm Gladwellian question—why do maids in Gurgaon never want to cook but only clean?

Cooking pays more money. Cooking is often less strenuous physical work. "But the reprimand that a maid receives for cooking something wrong or badly is far more than the reprimand for washing something wrongly or leaving the floor dirty."

To be at the office of The Maids' Company is to stand at the fault line of India's class war; behind me on the company's soft board stretch the names of buildings that define the dream of a town—South City, Aralias, Magnolias, Palm South City, West-end Heights, Pinnacle, Central Park, Princeton Estate, Wellington Estate. The residents wanted a piece of America, and though the town has failed them in many ways, they hold on to the promises made to them, trapped by the nomenclature.

One of the biggest problems Singh faced in the first few months is that maids would be dropped at the gate of the apartment block by the office van but would not reach the flat. "Many of them were very scared of elevators. They had never travelled in such (to them) magnificent, enclosed, silently swishing-away spaces. Some pressed the wrong button and went somewhere else—then panicked. It was literally out of this world for them," says Singh.

One day I went to The Maids' Company on their payday—usually the first Sunday of the month. As I entered, a shy middle-aged lady called Jogmaya, as employee of the month, got a present—fabric to stitch a new *salwar kameez*. Then a voice on the CD player sang, *"Blue hai paani, paani, paani, paani, paani; aur din bhi sunny, sunny, sunny, sunny..."* and the women danced, mimicking Bollywood actresses with oomph-y expressions. They dragged Singh to the dance floor. She was lithe and beautiful in a sari, making sharp moves that were a cross between hip-hop and bhangra. The coffee mug she left behind on the table beside me said, *Super Kudi*—"Super Girl" in Punjabi.

CHAPTER 6

MODELS IN VILLAGES

The cow peed in riverine spurts, sloshing pale urine that seeped into the dust, making it dark. "See—turning like chocolate color," said the man beside me happily. Srikant Bangar, 30, stared at his cow with the kind of unadulterated affection Lord Emsworth bestowed on the Empress of Blandings in P. G. Wodehouse's novels.

I am in Hiware Bazar,[1] a six-hour drive from India's financial capital, Bombay. To travel to Hiware Bazar, one drives out—preferably at first light as I did, to avoid the paralyzing Bombay traffic—along the Bombay-Pune highway for about three hours. This is one of the best expressways in the country and was India's first six-lane highway when it opened in 2002.

The road snakes across the Sahyadri mountain range on the Western Ghats, and on a good day, you can do the trip from Bombay to the university and automobile town of Pune in two hours flat. For years it was one of the few pieces of infrastructure that India could be proud of, but the month I went to Hiware Bazar, the expressway was in the news for the wrong reasons.

The pitch of protests against illegal and usurious toll collection—more than Rs 500 for one round trip to Pune—had reached violent levels. Two prominent opposition parties, the Shiv Sena and the Maharashtra Navnirman Sena, had asked its supporters not to pay the toll. This often translated into riotous attacks on toll booths by party activists. Some research showed that travelers were being charged thousands of crores more than what they should pay through illegal tolls imposed by a nexus of government leaders and real estate developers.

But even so, travel on the expressway is one of the few, and very far between, pleasures of good public infrastructure in India. From Pune, Hiware Bazar is another nearly three-hour drive toward the town of Ahmednagar—the village is located just before the town. This road is like the old highways of India, crowded and often pockmarked—none of it resembles the Bombay-Pune expressway corridor.

A few kilometers before Ahmednagar, the car turns into a small lane and then into fields in places where roads don't exist at all. All very classic rural India until all of a sudden, a few meters from the village, a well-paved, bump-free road pops up again. This leads straight into a village that, in fact, does not seem like an Indian village at all.

The roads are paved and almost entirely pothole free. In fact, they are far better than almost any road I have seen in Bombay. There are no open drains, no garbage dumped at corners, no dirty buzzing flies, no filthy puddles and no stench.

As an Indian, with years of having traveled in and visited Indian villages—often utterly foul and despondent places—coming to Hiware Bazar is almost surreal. In a country where nearly 400 million people, most of them in Indian villages, have never had electricity, Bangar's cowshed—in fact, every cowshed in the village—has solar-powered lighting. So do all its dozen or so temples and the one mosque that villagers built for the only Muslim family in the area.

In a country where no one who can afford not to drinks water straight from the tap—since 80 percent of the sewage never gets treated and much of it seeps into drinking-water sources like groundwater and rivers—at Hiware Bazar, it is entirely safe to drink straight from the tube wells. I did.

The village office, two-storied and white-washed twice each year, looks better than most government offices in Bombay. Its toilets are cleaner; the Internet connection on its computers is steady rather than patchy.

Standing beside his seven cows, Srikant Bangar told me that in recent months the village council had run a little contest—spot a mosquito and win Rs 500. "Most villages are full of mosquitoes because there is water and garbage collected everywhere," said Bangar. "But we don't have that here—no stale water, no mosquitoes!"

The contest may be apocryphal, but it points to a larger tale of Hiware Bazar and what it has achieved in the last two decades. When Bangar was a child, he remembers "people fighting in the village all the time." Until 1990, brewing local hooch was the main business in Hiware Bazar, once the home of some of the best traditional wrestlers in the country. More than 90 percent of the villagers lived in poverty, under the official poverty line that marks those in need of state support, and violent crime was common.

Habib Sayed, from the only Muslim family in the village, told me, "Before 1990, when the police came to intervene in a fight, often they were beaten by drunken villagers and sent away. Many of the wrestlers had gone to seed, had become musclemen and alcohol makers. Sometimes the local police were so scared that they refused to come. Every day there would be big fights. Some would use knives, some axes or sticks, whatever they could find."

This would have been disastrous in any community; in Hiware Bazar, it destroyed everything. To understand why, you must understand the location of the village—it lies in central Maharashtra, in Vidarbha, the drought-prone heart of India's most prosperous state.

Vidarbha has some of the worst droughts—and the most terrible rates of suicide among farmers maddened by poverty and debt. It is sometimes referred to as the heartland of India's farmer suicide crisis—where, according to some calculations, one farmer has killed himself each half hour for at least a decade. In 2011, the suicide rate among farmers was higher by 47 percent than among the rest of Indians. Even as I write this, five million farming families face drought, penury and starvation in Vidarbha.

In 1990, Hiware Bazar was so feared that no teacher was willing to join the government school. Its literacy level was barely 30 percent, well below the 45 percent national average.

To see what has changed since then, consider the numbers. In 1991, there were 180 families living in the village—this went up to 236 by 2011. There were 168 families below the poverty line in 1991—only three families remain at such low income levels. There were 22 landless families in 1991; by 2011 there were only six.

Per capita income rose from Rs 832 to more than Rs 30,000. Bangar's own family was making around Rs 50,000 ($843) a year—now they make around Rs 10 lakhs ($16,000). Their cattle produce nearly 100 liters (26.42 gallons) of milk every day. "Just from the sale of milk, we make around Rs 75,000 a month," said Bangar.

In 1991, Hiware Bazar had no health facilities—now it has a proper health-care facility with round-the-clock doctors and a well-stocked clinic. The village school, which previously taught (when it could even get teachers) only till Class 4 now teaches till Class 10. Literacy rates have improved vastly, from 30 percent to 95 percent.

Groundwater level, which had fallen to between 90 and 120 feet in 1991, has risen to between 15 and 40 feet; the area under irrigation has risen too, from 125 hectares (308 acres) to 650 hectares (1,606 acres). At the peak of summer in this rain-deprived region, the area under cultivation used to be barely 1 or 2 hectares (2.5 or 4.9 acres). This has grown to around 80 hectares (198 acres). Cropping intensity (the ratio between net area sown and total area cropped) has grown from 94 percent to 164 percent and the number of dug wells from 97 to 284.

Previously, the village had not a single hectare under drip irrigation—a critical, water-saving technique in water-deprived areas—but now it has 250 hectares (618 acres) under drip irrigation.

The number of milk-producing cattle has grown more than six-fold—from under 100 to 650. And milk production has grown from 150 liters (about 40 gallons) a day to 3,500 liters (about 925 gallons). What helps the milk production is the availability of good-quality grass, which went up from 100 metric tons (110 short tons) in 2000 to 6,000 metric tons (6,613 short tons) in 2004 and has since grown multifold.

The 977-hectare (2,414-acre) Hiware Bazar symbolizes how we can turn around everything that has gone wrong in Indian agriculture. Its key problem was universal to Indian farming—water. Most of Indian agriculture is rain fed. In large parts of the country, and especially in Maharashtra, water retention tends to be low because of geology—a lot of basalt rock. How to retain, manage and deploy water efficiently remains the biggest challenge of the Indian farmer. For years, and in the absence of a sustained push toward drip irrigation and having desecrated the old systems of water harvesting and cropping appropriate to water availability, farmers have pumped and dug deeper and deeper for water. In the next two decades, World Bank data shows, 60 percent of all aquifers in India will be in a critical condition of contamination and over exploited. This is because India is the largest user of groundwater in the world—around 230 cubic kilometers (about 55 cubic miles) a year, or a quarter of the global use of groundwater.

But all of this began to change in 1990 when a man called Popatrao Pawar, whose own father was a well-known local wrestler, became the *sarpanch,* or the head man, in the village elections. Pawar was barely in his late 20s then and had just about received his MCom (masters in commerce) degree from Pune University. He began a process of completely changing the way Hiware Bazar had looked at its water resources.

When I met Pawar, I asked him if he was thinking like an entrepreneur when he began his work. He laughed and said, "At least I had the problem that every start-up has—my family and friends told me this was utter stupidity and I should get a good job in the city."

Pawar said he spotted the key to the village's problem. "We had to convert our most precious resource—water. Everything else flowed from there."

So he got the people of the village together and decided to use government grants and funds for village water conservation projects. A watershed is a place that drains water to a common spot. When rainwater gathers in a watershed, it flows out in drainage lines. But if there is no vegetation or forest cover, the rainwater seeps off the land rapidly, carrying rich topsoil with it.

Using government funds, Pawar repaired 70 hectares (173 acres) of forest lands in and around the hillocks surrounding the village. Volunteer labor from the village helped create 40,000 contour trenches on the hills. A re-plantation drive that began then has added more than 100,000 trees to the village. The results were evident by 1993. "Right after the monsoons, many wells which had not seen water in years filled up," says Pawar. That year total irrigated area also rose from 20 hectares (49 acres) to 70 hectares (173 acres). By 1994, the village had its own five-year plan for regeneration built on some key principles—a ban on liquor and on cutting trees and unchecked grazing; added to that were family planning and volunteer labor by villagers in development work. Pawar and his associates like Sayed convinced 22 villagers to donate their personal land to expand the local school.

Around 660 water-harvesting structures were built, with contours to stop the runoff of rainwater across 414 hectares (1,023 acres); 70 hectares (173 acres) of regenerated forests began to recharge the wells. In all, in the first few years Pawar spent around Rs 42 lakhs of government money on fixing 1,000 critical hectares (2,471 acres). Grazing of cattle on watershed development land was banned, as was cutting trees except on private land for fuel. Bore wells were banned except two for drinking water to control the extraction of groundwater. Also forbidden was growing water-intensive crops like sugarcane and banana; instead, horticulture and vegetables like potatoes, tomatoes and onions are now grown successfully. In Hiware Bazar only 0.5 acres of sugarcane per farm can be grown as fodder, and drip irrigation is mandatory.

To improve health, the village also decided to stop using wood-fueled open earth ovens or *chullahs*. Instead, small biogas plants that provide kitchen fuel have been set up alongside huts and cattle sheds. Open defecation—a curse of Indian villages that causes disease—has been totally eliminated. Every house has toilets.

"I worked on the principle of return on investment. I told the government officers that if we can fix this village, it will become a model for the whole country, and I told the villagers that this was the only thing that could totally transform their lives. The ROI, as they said, was unbeatable," says Pawar, whose work has won Hiware Bazar, which gets a meager annual rainfall of only 300 to 400 millimeters (12 to 16 inches), 700 awards from the state and national government.

Pawar says that handing the water resources of the village to its women has really helped. "We realized that the biggest victims of the water crisis are women who often had to travel miles to get water for their homes, but since we started 'water budgeting,' it is the village women who determine everything and fine anyone who uses more than their quota of water," he said. Depending on the rainfall in a particular year, water is allocated for various uses starting with drinking water for villagers and cattle.

Rameshrao Pawar (no relation to Popatrao) is one of the biggest beneficiaries of Hiware Bazar's success. From an annual income of less than Rs 1 lakh, he now earns around Rs 30 lakhs. He says he does not think of himself as a farmer anymore but as an entrepreneur. "Farming is in deep crisis in India because the farmer does not think of himself as an entrepreneur, with clear growth, revenue and profit targets," says Rameshrao. He says none of it could have been done without a sense of equity. For instance, to start with, there were 22 landless families in the village. Typically all the groundwater belonged to the landowner, as did the grazing sites—so a landless farmer would have almost no incentive to participate in watershed projects or stop his cattle from free grazing. As the village has been able to irrigate and revitalize more and more of its land, plots for farming have been given to landless farmers. Even the remaining few landless families are about to receive land.

Both Rameshrao and Popatrao agree that the equity benefit and access to all is the core of their success story. "We agreed early on that community resources are for everyone. Water comes through rain—everyone has an equal right over it. Depending on how large the farm is, proportionally everyone would get water, without exception," says Popatrao.

To keep the village unpolluted, Hiware Bazar decided in 2008 that no one would use cars on village roads (even though they are one of the few villages in India whose roads can effortlessly handle any car)—only cycles and motorbikes. Cars are used only to travel to other villages or towns.

Also, a few years ago, the village decided to make HIV tests for men and women mandatory before marriage. Each of these decisions has been taken in open-forum village meetings and with the complete consent of all villagers.

There are now nearly 60 households in the village that have rupee millionaires or that earn more than Rs 10 lakh (one million rupees). Popatrao Pawar has been made the head of the state Model Village Programme, a government department that aims to effect similar change across at least 100 villages in Vidarbha. He says he has narrowed down his "formula" into a two-year strategy that can alter villages. "We no longer need the two decades during which we experimented at Hiware Bazar. We now know what works and what doesn't. We can apply things like developing watersheds, paving roads, building toilets, preventing detrimental grazing within two years at each village," says Pawar, who once dreamed of playing cricket for the state team. One of his biggest achievements he says is the return of 93 families who had migrated to Bombay from the village but have returned in the last five years. "We are saving hundreds of liters from the Bombay water consumption," says Pawar, smiling.

Before I left, Habib Sayed showed me around the village and also showed me a series of before-and-after photos of the village. He then took me up a hillock on the border of the village. A snaking, scrubland path spiraled up and finally arrived at a "viewing point." A neat concrete shelter with a paved floor and a concrete roof opened to a sprawling view of the rolling hills that surround Hiware Bazar.

Standing there Sayed looked quietly at the distant village for a while and then said, "And they say villages are backward."

♦ ♦ ♦

THESE WORDS COULD HAVE COME FROM THE CHIEF MINISTER OF THE large central Indian state of Madhya Pradesh. In fact he said something similar to me: "When I became chief minister, people told me the only hope is to diminish agriculture. I used to say but can't we get growth through agriculture? They would laugh in my face," Shivraj Singh Chouhan told me.

Chief Minister Chouhan was hardly known across India until about two years ago. His fame, if any, was restricted to his sprawling central Indian state, which was known for poverty, farmer suicides, terrible infrastructure (including some of the worst roads in the country) and its *dacoit*-infested ravines.

Madhya Pradesh made up the "M" in BIMARU, the Indian acronym for lost-cause states. The word BIMARU comes from *bimar*, Hindi for "ill."

Then something wonderful happened. Madhya Pradesh became an agricultural powerhouse producing record tons of grains (mainly wheat) and delivering the unthinkable. Madhya Pradesh produced 19.46 million metric tons (21.45 million short tons) of grain in 2011–2012, a record jump of 19 percent or 16 million metric tons (17.64 short tons) from the 2010–2011 season. The state has achieved something that would have been unthinkable even a few years ago. It matches, and sometimes even beats, traditional "food basket" states like Haryana and Punjab and is one of the biggest contributors to the central government's pool for food security.

This has happened in a short time in the history of a state. In 2002–2003, Madhya Pradesh contributed barely 200,000 metric tons (220,462 short tons) to the central pool. By 2012, it produced 85,000,000 metric tons (93,697,000 short tons).

This kind of success must be considered in the context of what is happening in Indian agriculture. India's National Crime Record Bureau calculates that 270,940 farmers have killed themselves since 1995. Between 1995 and 2000, farmers committed suicide at the rate of 14,462 per year, and between 2001 and 2011, this went up to 16,743 per year. Lack of agrarian storage facilities and sheer neglect means that India wastes 40 million tons of wheat each year according to the "Global Food: Waste Not, Want Not" report (2013) of the Institution of Mechanical Engineers.[2]

How did Chouhan do it?

In a sense his model has been the reverse of the model in many other Indian states that are trying to industrialize and are moving people out of agriculture. "I realized that there can be high growth in agriculture too—and it would be impossible in a predominantly agrarian state to remove large numbers of people from farming. That would be a disaster."

India's leading agriculture activist, Devinder Sharma, says Chouhan realized that forced industrialization would only create "agricultural refugees, who would struggle to find jobs in towns and cities. And they had no skills to help them find and keep those jobs. Also, the towns and cities of Madhya Pradesh—as is true for most of India—don't have the capacity to take in millions of new people who are in essence refugees."

Chouhan won a record third five-year term as chief minister in 2013 and in his first decade in power pushed the area under irrigation from one million hectares (2,471,053 acres) in 2004 to 2.5 million hectares (6,177,635 acres) by 2013. In 2012 alone, his government gave out Rs 9,000 crore ($1.5 billion) to three million farmers in the state as zero-interest loans. Madhya Pradesh has been steadily decreasing the rate of interest on government-provided

agricultural loans from about 15 to 16 percent when Chouhan
came to power in 2005 to 7 percent in 2003, 5 percent in 2008
and 3 percent in 2010. By 2012, it hit zero. These loans are largely
given to farmers to buy seeds and farming implements.

"Madhya Pradesh showed the way for constructive government intervention at a time when the microfinance institutions were charging anything between 24 and 36 percent," says
Devinder Sharma.

"It was a huge sigh of relief and showed Chouhan as a
pioneer."

The zero-percent loans have also raised the percentage of loan
recovery in agriculture, hitting an all-time high of 78 percent in
2012, with 4.5 million farmers who had Kisan Credit Cards or
agrarian loan cards. Loans were given to farmers to buy cattle
and drip irrigation facilities. And—in a simple but much-needed
intervention—when they brought their produce to the bazaar, it
was weighed by electronic weighing machines that were much
more accurate and tamper proof compared to the old mechanical machines. A digital records system was created that had a
bank of 1.5 million farmers with details of their landholdings,
bank accounts, mobile numbers and preferred procurement centers for the process of government purchase of grain at a minimum support price. This has helped grain procurement levels
jump from 4.9 million metric tons (5.4 million short tons) in
2003 to 12.7 million metric tons (14 short tons) in 2012. The
other big factor has been fixing the electricity supply to farms.
Chouhan has separated agriculture power feeders from industrial
ones, waived off Rs 1,800 crore ($303 million) in pending power
bills of agriculture consumers, and ensured at least ten hours of
uninterrupted power supply a day. The power supplied to agriculture was 6,776 million units in 2009; it increased to 9,478

million units in 2012–2013, a jump of 40 percent. Warehousing improved too—from 7.9 million metric tons (8.7 million short tons) in 2010–2011 to 11.5 million metric tons (12.68 short tons) in 2013–2014, with an aim of reaching 15 million metric tons (16.5 million short tons) in 2014–2015 (which if achieved would be higher than in any other state). Madhya Pradesh is the first state in the country to use silo bags to store grain.

In 2008, Chouhan, 52, who is the son of a poor farmer and who won a gold medal in philosophy for his master's degree, made one of his greatest moves in agriculture by giving a Rs 100 bonus per quintal of wheat procured above and apart from the central government–determined minimum support price. This was raised in 2013 to Rs 150.

Chouhan's agriculture production commissioner Madan Mohan Upadhyay explains it best.

"He is a hardcore farmer," says Upadhyay. "He came in with a pure focus—most people work in agriculture in this state, so growth has to be agriculture driven first and then expand to industry."

Even in farmer suicides, although Madhya Pradesh is among the top five states according to the National Crime Record Bureau, statistics show that the number of such cases has been steadily falling in the state. The bureau records that farmer suicides fell by 8 percent between 2009 and 2010 due to the sharp fall in two states—Madhya Pradesh and Chhattisgarh.

In 2012–2013, Madhya Pradesh beat Bihar to become the fastest-growing major Indian state according to data from the Central Statistics Office (CSO). The state grew 14.28 percent in agriculture (at a time when overall agricultural growth in India has been growing at the level of barely 3 percent a year for the last three decades), and its state gross domestic product (GSDP) grew by 10.02 percent.

In 2011–2012, Bihar topped the charts with 13.26 percent GSDP growth, and Madhya Pradesh came second at 11.81 percent, but in 2012–2013, Bihar's GSDP growth fell to 9.48 percent. Per capita income in Madhya Pradesh rose by 8.69 percent in 2012–2013.

In fact, surrounded by deeply indebted states like Uttar Pradesh and Punjab, Madhya Pradesh's net debt as a percentage of GSDP has fallen to 21.7 percent from 33 percent in the last six years, while percentage of interest payment as a percentage of revenue receipts has reduced from 15 percent to 9 percent in the last six years.

This performance is no fluke. In 2010–2011, agriculture in Madhya Pradesh grew by 9 percent. In 2009–2010, when the state got 35 percent less rainfall than usual, agrarian growth was still 7.2 percent. In the same period, industrial growth was one of the highest in India at 10.1 percent, though from a smaller base since 80 percent of the people still work in agriculture.

The chief minister says he had a long-term strategy when he started by focusing on agriculture. "If you look at history, the development has always happened first and most expansively at coastal areas, with ports like Maharashtra, Tamil Nadu, Bengal, but we are a landlocked state. So what do we do?

"So focus on agriculture first. Our aim is to become the wheat bowl of the country, why should it only be Punjab? As I keep telling people, take wheat from us, we are centrally located and therefore it is easier to transport to any area in India. We are a natural road transport hub. And if we produce a lot of food, it is a win-win for the whole country because food can be transported to any part quickly from the center."

Madan Mohan Upadhyay, who was also the former health secretary of the state, says he understood the chief minister's mindset when, in one of the first meetings, Chouhan, the father of two sons, described how in his childhood village he saw women struggling and even dying in childbirth. From that gruesome experience was born his innovative policy decision to start a Janani Express—a helpline in every district of Madhya Pradesh, where any woman about to give birth could call for a government ambulance to fetch her to the nearest hospital.

Chief Secretary R. Parasuram says the chief minister draws his policies deeply from his personal experiences. "This is why you will never see him in denial about female infanticide in MP (and why one of the biggest schemes of the government is on female infanticide)."

Madhya Pradesh is one of the worst offenders in declining sex ratio. This happens in India because some girl children are killed by parents in the womb or shortly after birth. One of the parents' main fears is the dowry that would have to be paid to a groom's family during the marriage of a daughter. That's why Chouhan has also started a scheme where he plays father of the bride in mass weddings organized by the state for poor girls, who are given Rs 15,000 when they get married. The chief minister himself gives them away, often at a scale of thousands in one go. This is one of the reasons why he has earned the nickname "Mamu" or maternal uncle in the state since giving away the bride is often a role played by maternal uncles in the absence of the father.

The chief minister says that for him policy starts at home. "Most people don't know that I have nine adopted daughters."

Some of the biggest beneficiaries of these schemes are farmers since villages have the highest rates of female infanticide and lack of hospital facilities—and so once again agriculture gets empowered in the state.

His efforts have won Madhya Pradesh the national agriculture prize, the Krishi Karman Samman, twice in a row. In 2012–2013,

Madhya Pradesh produced 27.7 million metric tons (30.5 million short tons) of grain, including 16.1 million metric tons (17.75 million short tons) of wheat. Madhya Pradesh now contributes 11.2 percent of India's total food grain production, 17.5 percent of India's total wheat production and 28.65 percent of its total pulses production. Madhya Pradesh surpassed other prominent agricultural states in India including Uttar Pradesh, Punjab, Andhra Pradesh, West Bengal, Haryana, Rajasthan, Maharashtra, Karnataka and Bihar in the category of states producing over 10 million metric tons (11.02 million short tons) of food grain in every aspect from production of grains to increase in yield.

"We wanted to prove that agriculture—which everyone seems to have given up on in India—can be reinvented. There can be a business model in agriculture too," Chouhan told me. "To do this, I began to rethink farming as a sustainable and growing, very profitable business which has maximum community impact and every farmer as a single business unit, as a successful social entrepreneur."

CHAPTER 7

THE NOT UNTOUCHABLES

Kalpana Saroj was 15 years old, or perhaps 16—she does not accurately remember—when she drank three bottles of pesticide. It would, she hoped, do exactly what she wanted: kill her.

For 24 hours Saroj, who now owns a Rs 250 crore ($42 million) empire that stretches from sugar to real estate to industrial pipes to movies, seemed to have slipped into a coma even as doctors at the local hospital near her native Roperkheda village in Vidarbha, the drought-ridden heart of the western state of Maharashtra, struggled to wash the poison out of her stomach. Then, just as suddenly and beating tremendous odds, she began to awaken.

She was only 15, but by that time she had been married, abused and tortured. She had spent nearly two years waking up every morning at 4:00 a.m. and working nearly nonstop apart from short breaks for meals and a bath (sometimes not even that) till midnight. She did not mind the cooking or the cleaning. Nor the hours of washing clothes.

But her husband's family kept chickens. Those cages would be full of chicken shit. "I had never seen such filth. The smell was horrible. I would vomit several times while trying to clean them," remembers Saroj.

Her police constable father had sent her to school until Class 10; he had hoped she would, even after marriage, be able to go to college. "He never wanted me to get married so early," says Saroj, now 53, who speaks fast, and starts answering before questions are completed. It is as if, decades after it all happened, the torture is embedded and alive, and sometimes even kicking.

She speaks casually, with only the slightly unnatural speed perhaps giving away the old pain, and every now and again there is a small pause as she stops to force herself to remember. During those months, she was given food only once or twice a day; often the smell of the chicken pens so nauseated her that she could not eat for days.

One day, about two years after her marriage, Saroj's father came to see her. "He was shocked. He had never seen me so shattered. He told my in-laws, 'I married off my daughter, I did not sell her into slavery,'" says Saroj. That day she returned to her father's house.

A new ordeal began. "I was a Dalit girl who had already broken her marriage. It was the biggest curse," says Saroj. Dalit literally means "oppressed" in Hindi. In the Hindu system of caste, the origins of which are disputed but whose poisonous effects have continued for centuries, for many Indians, Dalits are literally untouchables. They make up around 16 percent of the Indian population but have traditionally remained the lowest rung of society (the highest were the Brahmins). The Brahmins and other upper castes would not accept either food or water from the hand of a Dalit. They would not visit the homes of Dalits and would not invite a Dalit to their home. My grandmother had a phrase for the impossible situation that Dalits faced in the old days—*Bamnar aage hathleo dosh, pore hathleo dosh*. It means there is a problem if you walk before the Brahmin and there is a problem if you walk behind the Brahmin. It was meant to suggest the absolute farcical hopelessness of a situation. The Dalit could not walk in front of the Brahmin because an untouchable did not dare to be in front of the priestly caste—nor could the Dalit walk behind the Brahmin because he risked stepping on the shadow of the Brahmin, which was utterly unthinkable.

Even today in parts of India, the punishment meted out to an "errant" Dalit woman is to be paraded naked through the village—and often gang-raped by upper-caste men. In 2012, 33,655 crimes were committed against "scheduled castes," a government term for lower castes; the brunt of the violence is always directed toward Dalits.

All of this is in spite of the fact that the legal ban against caste discrimination was first introduced by the British in 1850 under the Caste Disabilities Removal Act (or Act XXI); special protection was then given to lower castes under the Government of India Act of 1935, and 17 separate laws were passed by various Indian states to end caste discrimination between 1943 and 1950. The first national legislation against caste discrimination in independent India (after 1947) was created with the Untouchability (Offenses) Act of 1955, which was strengthened in 1976 and made the Protection of Civil Rights Act. In 1990, a special law called the Scheduled Castes and Scheduled Tribes (Prevention of Atrocities) Act came into being. But the violence continues—and rates of violence doubled from around 14,000 in 1981 to 33,000 in 2001 and have remained stubbornly at those levels since then.

As India has modernized and urbanized, the most horrific of these crimes tend to take place in villages rather than in the big city where anonymity and modernity increasingly blur caste identity markers. Nearly all the women killed as "witches" each year in India (760 women have been killed since 2008 after being termed "witches" and 119 murdered in 2012 alone) were Dalits, and the majority of these hunts happened in the most rural states of India—Jharkhand and Odisha.

It is as if modern India is bringing alive with a vengeance what Bhimrao Ramji Ambedkar saw in the early twentieth century. Ambedkar, a Dalit scholar who was one of the finest intellectuals India has ever known, wrote the Indian constitution. A seminal figure in India's struggle for freedom from British rule, Ambedkar embraced the modern early. A graduate in law, economics and political science of Columbia University and the London School of Economics, he was a prodigious student. In his three years at Columbia, he took eleven courses in history, five in philosophy, three in politics, four in anthropology, one each in basic German and French and twenty-nine in economics. Ambedkar advocated the total destruction of the caste system and promoted inter-caste marriage. Barely weeks before his death in 1956, faced with unrelenting orthodox Hindu resistance and after years of research, he embraced Buddhism and urged Dalits to do the same. This kind of renouncing was not new in Ambedkar's politics and polemic. In November 1948, barely a year after independence, at a time when most Indians lived in villages and earned their living from farming, when Mahatma Gandhi made villages the cornerstone of his political philosophy and the prime unit of his idyllic Indian society, Ambedkar famously argued, "What is a village but a sink of localism, a den of ignorance, narrow mindedness and communalism."[1]

This is what Saroj faced when she returned to her father's village. Whispers started, asking why a Dalit girl had to leave her husband's home. Fingers were pointed at her father—had he failed to reveal some illicit fact about his daughter that was later unearthed by the in-laws?

"I could not take the insult of my father. I was convinced that the only way was to remove myself. I had to kill myself." Three bottles of pesticide later, she was alive but with the additional burden of a girl who had tried to kill herself. The gossip in the village asked if she was mad, if that's why she had been "sent back from her husband's home."

She then decided to do what Ambedkar wanted of Dalits—to leave the village and seek their fortune in the city. "But my parents and relatives did not want a young girl to come to the city. A girl who had left her husband, a girl who had no male guardian—it was unbelievable," remembers Saroj. "But I had crossed the final line—I was ready to die, so nothing could scare me anymore. I told them if they did not let me go, I would jump under a train and kill myself. And this time, there would be no time for doctors or hospitals to save me."

So it was that Saroj came to Bombay, the financial capital of India, to live with the family of a distant relative. Bombay, she says, seemed like America to her. It was dazzling and different from anything she had ever imagined. "I had never seen such tall buildings. In fact I didn't believe that buildings could be that tall," she says. "When I first saw the buildings of Mumbai [Bombay], I felt very scared but I also felt free. I had broken away from the shackles of the village. And even though I had failed to become a nurse or join the police like my father—or even join the military as I had hoped after my suicide since I did not fear death anymore—I felt that this was a place where I could make something of my life."

Her first job was at a small stitching center with a salary of Rs 200 a month. The first day she went there, Saroj froze. "I had never seen men and women working side by side in my life. And I never thought someone would offer me a Rs 100 note in my life. Here someone was offering me Rs 200! It was unbelievable," she says. She rented a room for herself in one of Bombay's slums—for Rs 40 a month.

After a couple of years working at that center, Saroj started a not-for-profit to help women from impoverished backgrounds access government funds in order to start small-scale enterprises. Soon she spotted a loan she could take (of Rs 50,000) and started a furniture shop. As business grew, Saroj became more entrenched in local politics. As she says, "Many people began to see me as someone who could get things done."

It was at this time, around 1996, that she was offered a plot of land of about two acres on a road that links the cities of Bombay and Pune. The asking price was Rs 2.5 lakhs and the owner wanted to sell only to Saroj. The land was filled with illegal encroachments of the local land mafia. "The owner told me—'Kalpana, I have two choices: either sell it to you and get Rs 2.5 lakhs, which is less than market value or give it up to the goons and get nothing,'" says Saroj.

This was the first deal that kick-started Saroj's career. But it was also the first time she was told that she might be killed—and when she decided to get her revolver license. The mafia put a price of Rs 10 lakh on her head. Saroj went to the home of the police commissioner and told him that she might be murdered. After months of legal battle, the land was cleared. On this she built her first commercial complex. She called it Kohinoor, after the famous Indian diamond.

Around this period, Saroj says she began to read Ambedkar's work very seriously. It made her question her concept of economics, and indeed her own life. Dalit economics in India has been the tale of the quota system, in essence a system of affirmative action where positions are reserved for the community in state-run schools and colleges and in government jobs. There has been endless debate, heartache and violence in India over these quotas. There is evidence that these quotas have been useful in some places to bring access to communities, but in many cases the reservation system has been overrun with rampant corruption and the worst kind of bureaucratic sloth. The quota system and the inclusion of various communities under the quota regime has also become a source of votes with political parties carving out "vote banks" by forcing the inclusion of different communities on the reservation benefit list.

There is also a raging debate over whether Ambedkar was a free-market proponent or a Fabian socialist, but it's undoubtedly clear that Ambedkar was far less anxious about private capital, enterprise and business than the men who came to govern independent India, including its first prime minister, Jawaharlal Nehru, an avowed socialist. In fact, Ambedkar opposed the inclusion of the word "socialist" in the constitution he wrote. On November 15, 1948, Ambedkar said in a constitutional debate,

> The constitution…is merely a mechanism for the purpose of regulating the work of the various organs of the state. It is not a mechanism whereby particular members or particular parties are installed in office. What should be the policy of the state, how the society should be organised in its social and economic side are matters which must be decided by the people themselves according to time and circumstances. It cannot be laid down in the constitution itself, because that is destroying democracy altogether. If you state in the constitution that the social organisation of the state shall take a particular form, you are, in my judgment, taking away the liberty of the people to decide what should be the social organisation in which they wish to live. It is perfectly possible today, for the majority of people to hold that the socialist organisation of society is better than the capitalist organisation of society. But it would be perfectly possible for thinking people to devise some other form of social organisation which might be better than the socialist organisation of today or of tomorrow. I do not see therefore why the constitution should tie down the people to live in a particular form and not leave it to the people themselves to decide it for themselves. This is one reason why the amendment should be opposed.

Ambedkar argued that the section in the constitution on the directive principles of state policy already included what he

thought were relevant guidelines about economic policy in Part
IV and Article 31, namely,

> The State shall, in particular, direct its policy towards securing-
>   (i) that the citizens, men and women equally, have the right to
>   an adequate means of livelihood;
> (ii) that the ownership and control of the material resources
>   of the community are so distributed as best to subserve the
>   common good;
> (iii) that the operation of the economic system does not result in
>   the concentration of wealth and means of production to the
>   common detriment;
> (iv) that there is equal pay for equal work for both men and
>   women.[2]

These Ambedkar thought were enough—there was no need to
bring in state ownership of capital, resources and industry, which
would curb private enterprise. Unlike many of his cabinet colleagues who were uninterested in economic theory, Ambedkar
wrote some of the most definitive works on economics in India.
This is a man who fervently spoke for industrialization and mechanization, and his ideals of socialism have more to do with justice
than with restricting the role of individual enterprise. His economic writings are replete with ideas that are being absorbed and
applied skillfully today by entrepreneurs like Saroj.

Ambedkar's three seminal works are *The Problem of the
Rupee: Its Origins and Solutions* (1923), *Administration and
Finance of the East India Company* (1915) and *The Evolution
of Provincial Finance in British India: A Study in the Provincial
Decentralisation of Imperial Finance* (1925).

Consider these two sections from *The Problem of the Rupee*:

Money is not only necessary to facilitate trade by obviating the difficulties of barter, but is also necessary to sustain production by permitting specialization. For, who would care to specialize if he could not trade his products for those of others which he wanted? Trade is the handmaid of production, and where the former cannot flourish the latter must languish. It is therefore evident that if a trading society is not to be out of gear and is not to forego the measureless advantages of its automatic adjustments in the great give-and-take of specialized industry, it must provide itself with a sound system of money.

Also,

Trade is an important apparatus in a society, based on private property and pursuit of individual gain; without it, it would be difficult for its members to distribute the specialized products of their labour. Surely a lottery or an administrative device would be incompatible with its nature. Indeed, if it is to preserve its character, the only mode for the necessary distribution of the products of separate industry is that of private trading. But a trading society is unavoidably a pecuniary society, a society which of necessity carries on its transactions in terms of money. In fact, the distribution is not primarily an exchange of products against products, but products against money. In such a society, money therefore necessarily becomes the pivot on which everything revolves. With money as the focusing-point of all human efforts, interests, desires, and ambitions, a trading society is bound to function in a regime of price, where successes and failures are results of nice calculations of price-outlay as against price-product.[3]

The economist in Ambedkar protested against the core ideas of the kind of state-driven socialism with which Jawaharlal Nehru would later be identified—a centralized, center-driven approach. Ambedkar wrote,

By centralisation all progress tends to be retarded, all initiative liable to be checked and the sense of responsibility of local authorities greatly impaired. Besides, centralisation involves and must involve a serious sacrifice of elasticity, for it is naturally disagreeable to a central department to have to deal with half a dozen different ways of managing the same branch of administration, and which therefore aims at reducing all types to one. Further centralisation conflicts with what may be regarded as a cardinal principle of good government, namely, that when administrative business reached an authority fully competent to deal with it, that authority should deal with it finally. Even when there is a higher authority equally competent, to pass the business on to it would at best help to transfer power to the hands of the tower ranks of the official hierarchy, by causing congestion of business in the Central Department...centralisation, unless greatly circumscribed, must lead to inefficiency. This was sure to occur even in homogeneous states, and above all in a country like India where there are to be found more diversities of race, language, religion, customs and economic conditions than in the whole continent of Europe. In such circumstances there must come a point at which the higher authority must be less competent than the tower, because it cannot by any possibility possess the requisite knowledge of all local conditions. It was therefore obvious that a central government for the whole of India could not be said to possess knowledge and experience of all various conditions prevailing in the different Provinces under it. It, therefore, necessarily became an authority less competent to deal with matters of provincial administration than the provincial governments, the members of which could not be said to be markedly inferior, and must generally be equal in ability to those of the central government, while necessarily superior as a body in point of knowledge.[4]

This is a critical point of departure from the overwhelming theme of Dalit empowerment in India, which has predominantly been driven by the central government and central laws. Yet in truth, political emancipation in the community has come from decentralization and devolution of power—whether through the rise of the Dravidian lower-caste parties in Tamil Nadu in the south or the rise of the Bahujan Samaj Party and other lower-caste political groupings in the northern heartland.

In a sense, the rise of Dalit entrepreneurship mirrors in the world of economics and commerce what has already happened in politics. Several Dalit entrepreneurs told me that the creation of the DICCI (Dalit Indian Chamber of Commerce and Industry) was an effort to push back against caste prejudice in the top tier of Indian business, which used to be dominated by upper-caste Gujarati Jains, Punjabis and Marwaris. DICCI now has 1,000 entrepreneur members—400 of these are in the western state of Maharashtra. It started with only 100 entrepreneurs in 2005. India's biggest industry lobbying group, CII (Confederation of Indian Industry), has announced that it will work with DICCI to propel the increased sourcing of goods and services from scheduled caste and scheduled tribe (SC and ST) entrepreneurs by 10 to 20 percent but, as Chandra Bhan Prasad, scholar and writer on Dalit issues, clarifies, only on merit.

For so long, the economic debate among Dalits has been simply what the appropriate level of central government largesse is. Now this clutch of feisty entrepreneurs was reclaiming Ambedkar's ideas and decentralizing the economic conversation.

One essay of Ambedkar's works that is rarely referred to fascinated me while I was writing this book. It is called *India on the Eve of the Crown Government*. Ambedkar begins by comparing the British Empire with the Roman Empire. The British, like the Romans, he says, based the ideology of their imperialism in the garb of the cultural betterment of those they conquer. He writes:

> They [the Romans] proclaimed that they were a people of superior race with a culture too high to be compared with any other, that they had a better system of administration, that they were versed in the arts of life. They also proclaimed that the rest were people of inferior race with a very low culture and were absolutely devoid of the arts of life, and that their administration was very despotic. As a logical consequence of this the Romans argued that it was their divine mission to civilise their low lying brethren, nay to conquer them and superimpose their culture in the name of humanity.[5]

Ambedkar objected to the British description of India as run by "brigands and despots" before the arrival of English civilization and quoted Sir Thomas Munro, who told British historians, "When we compare other countries with England, we usually speak of England as she now is, we scarcely ever think of going back beyond the Reformation and we are apt to regard every foreign country as ignorant and uncivilised, whose state of improvement does not in some degree approximate to our own, even though it should be higher than our own as at no distant period."[6] Ambedkar pointed out that the First Crusaders put 40,000 men, women and children to the sword during their conquest of Jerusalem. Who was the brigand then, Ambedkar asked, who the despot?

He then went on to do what he did best—analyze the prosperity of India and the Indians before the coming of the British. He particularly picked on British criticism of India's Muslim rulers:

We have a consensus of opinion on both Hindu and Mohomedan [Muslim] as regards the prosperity of India when the
Mohomedan conquest took place. The magnificence of Canouj
and the wealth of the Temple of Somnath bear witness to it. It
is a mistake to suppose that the Mussalman sovereigns of India
were barbarous and despots. On the other hand a majority
of them were men of extraordinary character. Mohommed of
Guzni showed so much munificence to individuals of eminence
that his capital exhibited a greater assemblage of literary genius
than any other monarch in Asia has ever been able to produce.
If rapacious in acquiring wealth, he was unrivalled in the judge-
ment and grandeur with which he knew how to expend it.

Of all his illustrious successors...Feroz Shah is very well
known for his administration. His public works consisted of
50 dams across rivers to promote irrigation, 40 mosques and
30 colleges, 100 Caravan series, 30 reservoirs, 100 hospitals,
100 public baths, 150 bridges, besides many other edifices for
pleasure and ornament; and, above all, the canal from the point
in the Jumna where it leaves the mountains of Carnal to Hausi
and Hissar, a work which has been partially restored by the
British Government. The historian of this monarch expatiates
on the happy state of the ryots under his Government, on the
goodness of their houses and furniture and the general use of
gold and silver ornaments amongst their women.... The general
state of the country must have been flourishing, for Milo de
Conti, an Italian traveller, who visited India about A.D. 1420,
speaks highly of what he saw in Guzerat, and found the banks
of the Ganges covered with towns amidst beautiful gardens
and orchards. He passed four famous cities before he reached
Maarazia, which he describes as a powerful city, filled with
gold, silver, and precious stones. His accounts are corroborated
by those of Barbora and Baitema, who travelled in the early

part of the sixteenth century. The former in particular describes Cambay as a remarkably well-built city, situated in a beautiful country, filled with merchants of all nations, and with artisans and manufacturers like those of Flanders. Caesar Frederic gives a similar account of Guzerat, and Ibne-Batuta, who travelled during the anarchy and oppression of Mohammed Tagluk's reign, in the middle of the fifteenth century, when insurrections were reigning in most parts of the country, enumerates many large and populous towns and cities, and gives a high impression of the state in which the country must have been before it fell into disorder. Baber (spelt nowadays as Babur), the founder of the Moghul dynasty in India found the country in a prosperous condition and was surprised at the immense population and the innumerable artisans everywhere. He was a benevolent ruler and public works marked his statesmanship. Sher Shah who temporarily wrested the throne from the Moghul was, excepting Akabar, the greatest of Mohomedan rulers and like Baber executed many public works.

Akbar's benevolent administration is too well known to need any mention.

The rule of Shah Jehan who reigned not so much as a king over his subjects, but rather as a father over his family was marked by the greatest prosperity; his reign was the most tranquil.

Speaking of the condition of the people in the dominions of the Marathas who were contemporaries of the later Moghuls a traveller says, "from Surat, I passed the ghats, and when I entered the country of the Maharattas, I thought myself in the midst of the simplicity and happiness of the golden age where nature was yet unchanged, and war and misery were unknown. The people were cheerful, vigorous, and in high health, and unbounded hospitality was a universal virtue; every door was open, and friends, neighbours and strangers, were alike wel-come to whatever they found."

With regard to the economic condition of the people in south-ern India which was under the rule of Tipoo, a historian says, "When a person, travelling through a strange country, finds it well cultivated, populous with industrious inhabitants, cities newly founded, commerce extending, towns increasing, and everything flourishing, so as to indicate happiness, he will naturally conclude it to be under a form of government congenial to the minds of the people. This is a picture of Tipoo's country, and this is our conclusion respecting its government....His government though strict and arbitrary, was the despotism of a strict and able sov-ereign, who nourishes, not oppresses, the subjects who are to be the means of his future aggrandisement, and his cruelties were, in general, inflicted on those who he considered as his enemies.

Clive described Bengal as a country of inexhaustible riches. Macaulay said, "In spite of the Mussalman despot and of the Maratha freebooter, Bengal was known through the East as the Garden of Eden—as the rich kingdom. Its population multiplied exceedingly; distant provinces were nourished from the over-flowing of its granaries: and the noble ladies of London and Paris were clothed in the delicate produce of its looms."[7]

But how did prosperous India become so poor? Ambedkar was clear about the answer. The British not only looted the enormous royal treasures of Indian kingdoms and principalities, but they also—even more dastardly in Ambedkar's eyes—killed Indian industry, trade and business through destructive economic policies.

The essay lists a range of such devastating shenanigans—from usurious duty structures to trade tariffs aimed at ruining Indian indus-try on everything from sugar to spice, cotton, coffee, gum and silk.

"All these" British discriminatory tactics, wrote Ambedkar, "were a means to kill Indian industries."

He quoted the nineteenth-century German-American economist Georg Friedrich List, who said, "Had they sanctioned the free importation into England of Indian cotton and silk goods, the English cotton and silk manufacturers must, of necessity, soon come to a stand. India had not only the advantage of cheaper labour and raw material, but also the experience, the skill and the practice of centuries."[8] He also cited Horace Hayman Wilson, the then renowned Indologist, who complained,

It is also a melancholy instance...of the wrong done to India by the country on which she has become dependent. It was stated in evidence (in 1813) that the cotton and silk goods of India up to the period could be sold for a profit in the British market at a price from 50 and 60 per cent lower than those fabricated in England. It consequently became necessary to protect the latter by duties of 70 and 80 per cent on their value, or by positive prohibition. Had this not been the case, had not such prohibitory duties and decrees existed, the mills of Paisley, and Manchester would have been stopped in their outset, and could scarcely have been again set in motion, even by the power of steam. They were created by the sacrifice of the Indian manufacture. Had India been independent, she would have retaliated, would have imposed prohibitive duties upon British goods, and would thus [have] preserved her own productive industry from annihilation. This act of self-defence was not permitted her. She was at the mercy of the stranger. British goods were forced upon her without paying duty, and the foreign manufacturer employed the arm of political injustice to keep down and ultimately strangle a competitor with whom he could not contend on equal terms.[9]

"Thus," said Ambedkar, "The prohibitory protectionist policy of England ruined the industries of the country whose wealth attracted these swarms of flies that drenched her to the last dregs."[10]

He concluded, "It is with industries ruined...over-taxed, with productivity too low to bear high taxes, with few avenues for display of native capacities, the people of India passed from the rule of the Company to the rule of the Crown."[11]

Yet, it is the native capacity today's Dalit entrepreneurs believe they are reviving. Saroj told me, "I had always been told that one could only get something in life if there was a quota [a reservation] for Dalits in that job or that education. That was my basic understanding—one needs quotas. All I wanted was a small, decently paying job—that would have made me happy. But I realized that Ambedkar wanted more for us."

And there is opportunity waiting to be tapped. Research done by the Harvard Business School shows that scheduled castes accounted for around 16.4 percent of the population (2001 census) but owned only 9.8 percent of all enterprises before 2005. The only nuance here is that while the numbers of enterprises may have grown, many of them are still one- or two-person projects. These are enterprises of desperation—due to the lack of job opportunities anywhere else—rather than entrepreneurship by choice.

But then, in a way, Kalpana Saroj also began as an entrepreneur of desperation—she would have been happy with a job in nursing or the police. She says it is not a distinction she makes. "I learnt from Ambedkar that opportunities are blessings for Dalits—it does not matter how they have come." It is a lesson that illuminates her life choices. By the time her first real estate project was completed and her sugar mill built, Saroj had received several death threats and had acquired her gun license. She says she was determined that if she was going to die, she would at least fire back.

Then came her big breakthrough—in 2006, employees of the once grand but by then ruined company Kamani Tubes approached her to buy out the company. There were 170 cases against the non-ferrous metal tubes and pipes maker and a debt of Rs 116 crores ($19 million). The Kamani family, whose name before independence was as big as the biggest business houses, like the Tatas and the Birlas, and whose founder once associated closely with Mahatma Gandhi, had given up control of the company to employees in 1997 after many years of labor trouble and family infighting.

When the company came to Saroj, she was astounded by its illustrious past. The founder, Ramjibhai Kamani, was the pioneer in electric power transmission in India and in the production of industrial materials like arsenical copper plates, cupronickel sheets and the manufacture of zinc oxide and lead oxide. In 1945, the Kamani Engineering Corporation (KEC) became the first electric power transmission company not just in India but in the whole of Asia; and in 1950 it built the transmission towers for the Bhakra Nangal dam project, one of the dream projects of Jawaharlal Nehru, who called big dams the temples of modern India. By the mid-1960s, KEC was making the majority of the transmission towers in India. The company also produced a special road roller that could be swiftly transported in trucks and used in mountain areas. By the 1970s, the Kamani Group had expanded from metals to rubber to chemicals and jewel bearings; 80 percent of its $13 million turnover was coming from exports, and it had become the world's second largest maker of transmission towers, behind only Italy's SAE. But the oil crisis in 1973 brought massive debt to KEC that was worsened by the energy crisis in 1979. By the mid-1980s, racked by infighting, the family was losing control. In the 1990s, when the employees tried to take over and run it, they succeeded only in running it further into the ground.

The company then came under the Board of Industrial and Financial Reconstruction (BIFR), which handles the rehabilitation of sick industrial units, who approached Saroj and asked her to present a plan for reviving the company to the BIFR. "Once again this was something I had never done before, a business that I really did not understand," says Saroj.

Over the years, the debt has been wiped out, the workers' dues cleared and the son of Ramjibhai has been given Rs 51 lakh as a settlement of old pension dues. One of the things Saroj got with this deal was a building in Ballard Estate, the toniest and most old-world business district in India. A hop and a skip away from Saroj's office—which is on a street named after Ramjibhai Kamani—is Tata House, home to the venerable House of Tatas, India's biggest business conglomerate. Nearby also is Maker Chambers and the office of India's most powerful man in business, the billionaire Mukesh Ambani, head of Reliance Industries, the country's biggest privately owned company.

Sitting in that four-story office, Saroj's daughter Seema told me that her proudest moment was in 2013 when her mother was awarded the Padma Shri, one of India's highest civilian awards.

"I don't think of myself in caste terms, but I know how that feels," Seema Saroj told me. She had lived with her mother in a large slum until she was in Class 10. Even today she lives in a three-bedroom apartment not far from her mother in the distant suburb of Ulhasnagar. They have the money to buy homes in south Bombay, where real estate is some of the most expensive in the world, but Kalpana refuses to do so and prefers the three-hour drive one way to her office. Sometimes she uses her Mercedes, sometimes the Toyota Fortuner. "My mother says her people are there in Ulhasnagar, they are the ones who have been there for her all these years. They turn to my mother whenever they need something. She can't leave them. They can't come looking for her in south Mumbai [Bombay]."

Seema Saroj is married to her college sweetheart, a Brahmin, who now works in the company. Was there trouble when they got married? A little bit, said Seema, from her husband's side. But when I later asked Kalpana Saroj this, she just laughed it off and said, "The journey to honor is a long one. I am happy that my son-in-law now works with me."

Sometimes, though, things don't fall into place. For instance, Kalpana Saroj just financed a film on the horrific Khairlanji murders of 2006 when a four-member Dalit family, the Bhotmanges, was butchered by upper-caste Hindus over a land dispute. As is almost always the case, the women were paraded naked in the village before being murdered. There was only one survivor, Bhaiyalal Bhotmange. Before the film was shown, Bhaiyalal signed a document saying he had no objections. But after he saw the film, he decided to go to court—because the film shows him consuming alcohol.

The case is in court—and Saroj has agreed to pay for the prosecutor's fees too since Bhaiyalal is very poor. "It will be a long journey," Seema Saroj echoed her mother. "But we are used to hurdles."

◆ ◆ ◆

THE JOURNEY MIGHT BE LONG, BUT USING ENTREPRENEURSHIP TO FIGHT it is a more recent phenomenon. In 2010, the Indian Institute of Dalit Studies tried to understand enterprise in the community through a study done in the states of Uttar Pradesh and Haryana, in the towns of Saharanpur and Panipat.[12]

This seminal research is invaluable in understanding where Dalits come from, why they start businesses and why Dalit entrepreneurship is today one of the biggest weapons against caste in India.

It points out that people belonging to India's 16 percent Dalit population have traditionally never owned land or any other income-generating assets. With increasing mechanization, the need for farm labor, one of the traditional occupations for Dalits, is thinning and self-employment is on the rise. Uttar Pradesh and Haryana were chosen for the survey because both of these states have high Dalit populations, more than 19 percent and 21 percent, respectively.

In two towns, the study mapped 321 Dalit enterprises of varying sizes. In the towns selected, Panipat (in Haryana) had one Dalit business before 1950 and Saharanpur (in Uttar Pradesh) had none. Between 1951 and 1960 there was one business started in Panipat but none in Saharanpur, which, however, got three new businesses between 1961 and 1970. There were five new businesses started in these two areas between 1971 and 1980; then came the first signs of a quantum jump: there were 32 in the following decade, 118 in the ten years after that and 161 since 2000. The research shows that social mobility came to the communities only when they were able to "consolidate themselves economically, which happened in most parts of north India during the 1980s." That's when "they developed the capacity to diversify into occupations other than those they had been traditionally employed in, except of course for the jobs in the government sector under the reservation quota."[13]

This is what social researcher Chandra Bhan Prasad's work had also shown—liberalization gave the Dalit community economic wings.

What kind of businesses did the Dalits start?

Most of them were simple enterprises based in localities where they lived. These ranged from small shops, hotels, workshops, dealerships or franchises, small factories, medical clinics, and so on. Of the seven women mapped by the study, six had small grocery shops; workshops, like automotive mechanical outfits, were another favorite.

So who were these Dalit entrepreneurs? Most of them were men, and a very small number were women. Nearly 80 percent were relatively young, between 20 and 40 years of age, and most of them were married and had families with five or six members. The other interesting thing was that less than one-fourth lived in joint families (with their parents and other relatives). This was particularly interesting because this means that Dalits from small towns were mirroring the trend across India of smaller, nuclear families, led by the biggest urban centers like Delhi and Bombay. Curiously, most of them said they were Hindus—even though the Dalit identity comes from the active Ambedkarite rejection of Hinduism. For many of the people who participated in the survey, this Hindu tag was more of a social thing than a religious affirmation, though some did tell the surveyors, "Even after all the insults for centuries, we are still carrying the burden of Hinduism."[14] This simply means they felt discriminated against by upper-caste Hindus and often trapped by tradition and discrimination based on birth.

Almost all of them were first-generation entrepreneurs, and about three-fourths had fathers who had worked as laborers. Some were in government jobs, no doubt fueled by quotas. The fathers were mostly illiterate or had received very little primary education. Most of the poorest and lowest-strata Dalits actually said that their fathers had worked in jobs like manual scavenging of human excreta—traditionally done by the lowest among the untouchables.

Most of the Dalits who had started the entrepreneurial journey had been born in or lived in urban areas—reaffirming Ambedkar's famous advice to leave the village to break caste chains.

Most of the Dalits who started businesses had had basic schooling and at least a third had been to college. Nearly a fourth had some sort of technical education or had received a diploma or a degree. Nearly half said they acquired the technical skills required for the business by working with someone who was already in a similar business. Many of them did not start out as entrepreneurs. About a third started as wage labor, some in government jobs, and almost everyone had started with very little capital. Nearly 41 percent started their business with an investment of Rs 25,000 ($421) or less, another 22 percent had invested more than Rs 25,000 but less than Rs 50,000. Some were lucky to have had about Rs 100,000 to spare to start a business, but that seemed to be the upper limit. The money had come mostly from savings or from loans from friends and family. Less than 20 percent of the people had taken a loan from a formal institution like a bank, and barely that many had done so after they had started their business. Now here's the interesting part, which gives another insight into the Dalit entrepreneur's mind: even though at least half of the entrepreneurs surveyed knew about special government loans for Dalits, many of them "either did not approach a bank out of some kind of cynicism or were simply refused a loan for want of a good reference or an asset against which the loan could be approved. Their caste background played a role"[15] in their reluctance to approach government agencies for funds for fear of humiliation.

So what motivated them to go into business? Some had no source of livelihood. Others saw a renewed sense of dignity in their new occupation. "It helped them move out of village and traditional caste based occupations."[16] One of the consistent responses in the survey was that it was better to do something on your own than to slave for someone else. They had been helped in the initial phases mostly by their families and friends—though at least a fourth claimed that they did not receive any help from anyone. Almost always their caste was the biggest barrier to getting started. Some could not find people who would rent them space; others could not find accommodation in or near the place where they wanted to start their business since most upper castes would not rent to them. This meant that most businesses were small in size and most of them were self-owned rather than partnerships. Half of the respondents owned the space where they started their business and the rest rented space. Half worked alone; others hired staff ranging from one person to more than 50.

Hiring non-Dalit staff is another classic problem of the Dalit entrepreneur. The good news is that the survey showed that almost all Dalit enterprises had grown—but the exact rate of growth was hazy since most did not maintain proper books. More than half had a small turnover—about Rs 100,000 ($1,686) or so a year. The number of those who reported annual turnover above a lakh of rupees was also significant with 28 percent reporting a turnover of 1 to 5 lakhs and another 6 percent reporting it to be between 5 and 50 lakhs. Two respondents reported a turnover of above 50 lakhs. The other big question is—where were Dalit businesses located? Since higher castes often do not want proximity to Dalits, a third of the Dalit businesses were located in areas with a majority Dalit population—in many cases they were extensions of their living quarters. But half of the respondents said they worked from mixed localities with a majority of non-Dalit population. Surprisingly, almost everyone said that they faced no discrimination at the location of their business, and they had no issues relating to their caste in the place of work.

In some cases, Dalits worked in traditional caste-related occupations like leather (since it involves handling dead animals). But newer opportunities had also opened up—in education, for instance. Especially in Uttar Pradesh, there are many Dalit-run schools. The best part about these Dalit-owned and Dalit-run private schools is that, when well run, they often had students from all castes, not just Dalits. In fact, the study found that only a small number (5 percent) of Dalit-run schools said that their students were only Dalits. A large majority, 78 percent, reported that students from all castes studied with them—breaking yet another major barrier.

In fact the key purpose of the study was to understand the "caste dimension of the everyday economic life in the regional urban context as it is experienced by those who come from the bottom line of caste hierarchy and have tried to step into areas of economic activities that have been hitherto closed to them for various social and historical reasons."[17] In essence, to understand how caste affects livelihood and the search for starting an enterprise.

In short, it asks—does caste matter?

It does, said 63 percent of the people who participated in this survey: they had faced some kind of discrimination in their lives. But interestingly, only 42 percent had faced discrimination in business—showing that entrepreneurship is one of those areas where the impact of caste is naturally lower.

How did caste matter in business?

Some said they were not acceptable to the larger business community. The study reported, "The locally dominant communities, who have traditionally dominated the business scene, do not like Dalits getting into business."[18] But interestingly, barely 5 percent had any trouble buying things—as long as you can pay, no one cares who you are!

One of the biggest problems that the Dalits faced was the lack of powerful social networks that would, for instance, help them access informal funds or stand guarantees for bank loans. "Banks ask for guarantee. We do not own expensive houses or plots of land in the city. Neither do we own any agricultural land. Our businesses are also small. Why would banks give us loans?"[19] said one respondent in the report.

One curious thing that the study found was that Dalit entrepreneurs often articulate caste discrimination also in terms of access to finance. Inevitably, most of them borrowed from family and friends. Their biggest problem is no different from the problem faced by most start-ups—lack of resources. The caste burden finally plays out, more often than not, as a resource crunch. One respondent said: "Our main problem is the lack of resources. Our people are poor and also lack confidence to come to cities and try something new. Even those who have the courage, fail to go far. This is because we lack social contacts."[20]

The key takeaway from the study was that almost all of Dalit entrepreneurs felt that they had made something of their lives. Through entrepreneurship they had found dignity, broken away from "a life of slavery" and received greater respect in society compared to their peers in the same community. Not only were they self-sufficient, many were even in a position to provide employment to others—which brought about an unprecedented sense of empowerment. In a sense, they had become "role models" in their community, and in turn pushed for the best education for their children.[21]

The one man who brought this study to life for me was Sunil Zode. I met him at a dinner to which Chandra Bhan Prasad invited me.

His (cryptic, without the right context) email invitation was titled—ABCD.

It read,

Dear Gated Queen-ed,

Probably indisputably, London isn't dated yet. It continues moderating modernity for the good of the globe.

London minus ABCD?

Shouldn't we reflect upon our own predicaments minus ABCD!

Please judge the man judiciously. He fathered ABCD on this part of the mother planet earth. But was he a mind-colonizer for the crown? Sure enough, he said the following:

We must at present do our best to form a class who may be interpreters between us and the millions whom we govern; a class of persons, Indian in blood and colour, but English in taste, in opinions, in morals, and in intellect.

Is the above half-truth or full falsehood? Consider the full text:

We must at present do our best to form a class who may be interpreters between us and the millions whom we govern; a class of persons, Indian in blood and colour, but English in taste, in opinions, in morals, and in intellect. To that class we may leave it to refine the vernacular dialects of the country, to enrich those dialects with terms of science borrowed from the Western nomenclature, and to render them by degrees fit vehicles for conveying knowledge to the great mass of the population.

Clearly, Indian history writers painted a liberator into a colonizer.

In the same Minutes on Education, Lord (Macaulay) said something very strange about his own country:

At that time almost everything that was worth reading was contained in the writings of the ancient Greeks and Romans. Had our ancestors acted as the Committee of Public Instruction has hitherto acted; had they neglected the language of Cicero and Tacitus; had they confined their attention to the old dialects of our own island; had they printed nothing and taught nothing at the universities but Chronicles in Anglo-Saxon, and Romances in Norman-French, would England have been what she now is? What the Greek and Latin were to the contemporaries of More and Ascham, our tongue is to the people of India.

Sure enough, Lord Macaulay was non-partisan.

We most humbly invite you to please join the dinner on the English Day and demand ABCD as fundamental rights to all Dalits born today onwards.

Food to be Tharoor Class and Liquid like Niagara Fall.

Time: 07 pm Onwards, Venue: Terrace Pergola, IIC Main Building.[22]

For the uninitiated, this is perplexing stuff, but it contains centuries of Indian politics hidden in one email. The "gated" reference is to Delhi's infamous elite class who live in gated colonies that are shut off every night—and have no passersby unless you live inside the colony.

The Macaulay mention lies at the heart of one of India's most bitter class divides—between those whose primary mode of schooling was in the English language and those who did not go to an "English-medium" school. Baron Thomas Babington Macaulay was a British historian and politician who supported the transfer of the official language of the government in India from Persian (favored by the old Mughal courts) to English in the mid-nineteenth century. In the years leading to the English Education Act of 1835, Macaulay wrote a "Minute upon Indian Education." It says all the things that the invitation from Prasad says it does.

It also says, "I have conversed both here and at home with men distinguished by their proficiency in the Eastern tongues....I have never found one among them who could deny that a single shelf of a good European library was worth the whole native literature of India and Arabia. Honours might be roughly even in works of the imagination, such as poetry, but when we pass from works of imagination to works in which facts are recorded, and general principles investigated, the superiority of the Europeans becomes absolutely immeasurable."[23]

It also says,

Whoever knows [English] has ready access to all the vast intellectual wealth, which all the wisest nations of the earth have created and hoarded in the course of ninety generations. It may be safely said, that the literature now extant in that language is of far greater value than all the literature which three hundred years ago was extant in all the languages of the world together.... The question now before us is simply whether, when it is in our power to teach this language, we shall teach languages, by which, by universal confession, there are not books on any subject which deserve to be compared to our own; whether, when we can teach European science, we shall teach systems which, by universal confession, whenever they differ from those of Europe, differ for the worse; and whether, when we can patronise sound philosophy and true history, we shall countenance, at the public expense, medical doctrines, which would disgrace an English farrier, astronomy, which would move laughter in girls at an English boarding school, history, abounding with kings thirty feet high, and reigns thirty thousand years long, and geography, made up of seas of treacle and seas of butter.[24]

Modern-day India has great disdain for "Macaulay's children," or Indians who proclaim superiority because of their knowledge of English—and the West. But Ambedkar—and even today's Dalits—have the reverse opinion. They realize, accurately, that English frees them, puts them on a par, gives them not just equality in society, but equanimity. While Sanskrit, the language of Hindu orthodoxy, and therefore caste bias, which could traditionally only be accessed by the Brahmins, keeps the lower castes trapped, English unlocks the chains.

Therefore this worship of Goddess English; therefore this party.

The divide comes from independence. Both Gandhi and Nehru were London-educated barristers, as was Muhammad Ali Jinnah, the leader of Pakistan's independence movement and the founder of the state of Pakistan. Over the years a feeling developed in India that it was a country ruled by a handful of British- (later American-) educated politicians who had little contact with the rest of India.

The reference to "Tharoor Class" is to Shashi Tharoor, the very suave former UN diplomat turned Congress Party Member of Parliament. Tharoor is a graduate of St Stephen's College, one of the most elite liberal arts colleges of India, and the alma mater of many members of the Congress Party which has ruled India for most of its modern history, including the latest scion of the Gandhi–Nehru family, the perpetual head of the Congress, Rahul Gandhi. Tharoor has a PhD from Tufts University in international relations, was a career diplomat rising to undersecretary general of the UN before he returned home to enter politics.

This is the divide that fuels today's India. What most people don't understand is that the caste divide is also the class divide— which is why economics, money, earnings and prosperity are often its most potent antidote in modern India.

This little party in Delhi to which Prasad invited me was to celebrate another Ambedkar lesson to his people—embrace English.

The hall where it was being held had a little iron statue of a woman carrying a book on one side. She was, I was told, the Goddess of English. "We worship her," said Prasad, "because she sets us free."

This is something Seema Saroj also says. The moment she starts to speak fluent English (her mother speaks the language only haltingly), something changes even among people who know her caste. "The barriers fall," she told me.

◆ ◆ ◆

SUNIL ZODE WAS HAVING A QUIET GLASS OF SWEET LIME AND SODA AT THE party when I met him. He caught me looking at his shoes, which had caught my eye for their dazzling polish. "I like good shoes and I polish them well. The first pair of shoes I ever wore, I had to steal them. I did not have money to buy shoes," said Zode.

There were many people that evening and we didn't get a chance to speak more, but later in Bombay where he lives, Zode told me his story. He owns six companies, including a large insecticides firm, a travel company and some logistics companies. His annual turnover is Rs 20 crores ($3.3 million).

He is the youngest of seven children born to an agricultural worker in the rural Wardha district of Maharashtra. Often there was no food to eat. Until Class 7, often he had only one set of clothes—and no shoes.

Around five years later, his eldest brother got some work at Mantralaya, the government secretariat in Bombay, and Zode, who had just finished school, joined his brother in the city, replicating that old lesson that the city often sets the Dalit free.

The brothers started a small poultry business in the satellite town of Alibaug. Soon business grew and Zode opened a gas agency in the area of Bombay called Byculla, which, then as in many parts now, was a mafia den.

"That's where I learnt the value of politeness and that in order to do business, you can never be the first one to get angry," he says.

When he married, he steered his microbiologist wife toward business and started Hindustan Insecticides. "For me, the lesson of Ambedkar is—never let an opportunity go to waste. We Dalits don't get that many opportunities," says Zode, who now lives in a Rs 4 crore ($674,000) home in tony Bandra in the heart of Bombay, and drives a C-class Mercedes to work.

But he didn't allow his son to go to America for a degree. "I was very clear—if you get admission to a top engineering college or a management institute in India, then you can go abroad. I will know that you have the capability to be the best. But if he can't crack that, then it is only my money that is sending him abroad—what is the point of that?" asks Zode.

He says that what he has done for his children is this: "When they come out of their Bandra home and meet their friends, no one calls out to them by their caste as they used to call to me and my siblings in our village."

CHAPTER 8

THE "PERVERT" PAD MAKER

"You know what I am, right?" Arunachalam Muruganantham told me. "I am a pervert. That's why my wife left me, my mother left me. They were scared that I have gone crazy."

But why did they think so?

"Because of all the things I was doing, you see. I was asking young college girls about their periods, I was asking them for sanitary napkins, I was asking them what works best in a sanitary napkin.

"Even my wife was reluctant to discuss all these things with me—so forget the other girls. But when I persisted, everyone thought I was mad, or a pervert. They told me go and get some treatment done!"

Then he laughed steadily for some time. He laughs in a curious way, as if in between the guffaws something is hurting him. In conversation, he says the most devastating things quickly followed by a joke. For instance, he will say—my wife left me. Then quickly say—sometimes I had to wear a sanitary pad myself to test it. Then laugh again.

Muruganantham is perhaps India's most radical entrepreneur. He would easily be one of the most radical in the world. He is 46 years old and is a Class 9 school dropout. Till about ten years ago, he was a workshop mechanic in the village of Pappanaickenpudur in the southern town of Coimbatore. He had what he calls the "idyllic, very poor life."

"I used to earn very little and later on when I learnt the phrase 'stay-at-home husband,' I thought that was the right description for me. So these days when someone asks me about that phase of my life, I say I was a stay-at-home husband," says Muruganantham.

Then something happened that transformed him into one of India's most cutting-edge innovators. What does he make? He created a machine that can make some of the cheapest but good-quality sanitary napkins in the world. It is a machine that has been sold in 1,300 locations in India and around the world including in Nepal, Bangladesh, the Philippines, Mauritius, Kenya, Nigeria, Ghana, South Africa, Mozambique and even America.

The total business done by all the units is around Rs 150 crores ($25 million) a year but Muruganantham makes very little of that money. He sells the machine for only Rs 75,000 ($1,264) each. His own unit in Coimbatore makes a turnover of only Rs 5 crore ($843,000) a year. His vision is that in every part of the world, low-cost sanitary napkins can be made and used until not a single woman anywhere in the world is without a pad when she needs one.

This for a machine for whose patent Muruganantham had to sell blood. His patent for the machine was pending at the Indian Institute of Technology when he was asked to return repeatedly for clarifications. On one such call, he realized that he did not have the money to travel from his village to Chennai—about 6 or 7 hours away. "I was a frequent blood donor. And that time, I realized that for once let me donate blood not because someone needs it but because I desperately need the money." He got Rs 200 for his donation, made the trip and got his patent.

This is a revolutionary achievement for an Indian man—especially with the means and background of Muruganantham. But more on that in a bit. First, let's look at why this kind of innovation is vital in a country like India.

Only about 12 percent of India's 355 million menstruating women use sanitary napkins, says a 2011 AC Nielsen and Plan India survey called "Sanitary Protection: Every Women's Health Right."[1] In 2010, the Ministry of Health announced a Rs 150 crore ($25 million) scheme to bring access to sanitary napkins to girls in rural areas, but the impact of the scheme is yet to be measured. The Plan India Survey conducted across 1,033 women of menstrual age and 151 gynecologists throughout India showed that improper menstrual protection makes adolescent girls (age group 12–18 years) miss five days of school in a month, and around 23 percent of these girls actually drop out of school after they start menstruating. The biggest challenge, said the survey, is affordability: around 70 percent of women cannot afford to buy pads.

Compared to India's 12 percent, in Japan and Singapore 100 percent of women use sanitary pads, as do 64 percent in China and 88 percent in Indonesia. Talking about menstrual health is largely difficult and full of societal taboo. In many places in India, menstruating women are kept away from temples and kitchens, and some don't even bathe. Gynecologists condemn such practices, suggesting that women who are menstruating should bathe more than twice a day and change sanitary towels thrice. Almost all gynecologists believe that the use of sanitary pads reduces the risk of disease, including cervical cancer. The survey conducted across the cities of Delhi, Chennai, Calcutta, Bangalore, Lucknow, Hyderabad, Gorakhpur, Aurangabad and Vijayawada showed that around 31 percent of women reported a drop in productivity levels during their periods. The situation was worst in eastern India, where 83 percent of the women spoken to said they could not afford sanitary napkins, and in northern India, where 30 percent of girls dropped out of school after hitting menstrual age.

One day in 1998, Muruganantham noticed his new wife sneaking past him to the bathroom carrying something in her hand. He asked her what it was. She wouldn't tell him and asked him to mind his own business.

"No matter how many times I asked her she wouldn't tell me. Then I noticed that it was a dirty piece of rag, so filthy that I wouldn't even use it for cleaning my machines in the workshop," says Muruganantham.

"I realized that she was using this cloth as her menstruating cloth."

So he asked his wife why she did not use a sanitary pad. Shanthi, his wife, told him that she couldn't afford it. "'Either it is milk or vegetables or my pad—we can't have all three,' she told me," says Muruganantham. "For the first time in my life, I felt very poor."

Muruganantham had some money saved up, so he took that and went to the nearby village shop to buy a sanitary pad for his wife. This was the first time in his life he had done two things—the first time he had discussed menstruation with anyone, let alone a woman, and the first time he had ever held a packet of sanitary pads in his hand. So he was amazed at how light it was. He says it immediately occurred to him that this was largely cotton wool.

"I calculated in my head that this much cotton wool would not cost more than 10 paisa—but the price was about Rs 4 per pad. It was a huge profit margin. In fact, I was amazed that there could be such a profit margin in something like sanitary pads," says he. That's when he decided that he wanted to make and sell sanitary pads. But there were critical hurdles.

For instance, he had no idea that menstruation was a monthly cycle. The first pad that was made by Muruganantham was given to Shanthi. She was asked to give feedback. "She slapped me on the head and told me that I was crazy. That was the first time that I got to know that this is a monthly cycle! But how would one know? Who talks about these things in an Indian village? That was also the beginning of people calling me mad."

The pad maker figured that if he depended on his wife alone as a testing volunteer, it would take years before he would be able to develop anything. But how would be ever be able to find other testing volunteers?

As he hunted for women who would test his products, Muruganantham began to research a problem he knew almost nothing about. He realized that in most parts of India, especially in rural India, menstrual hygiene is almost nonexistent. The branded sanitary napkins are either too expensive or there is no awareness that they even exist. Even if people know that napkins exist, most of them don't know why they are important. "I did not know that word at that time but I later learnt that I had discovered a new market, a barely penetrated market—all these big words I didn't know. I just knew that here was a product that was essential for good health and it was missing for most Indian women," he says. He also discovered that women were using not just dirty rags but even leaves and ash and sand as menstrual protection.

Medical research shows that almost three-fourths of all reproductive diseases in India come from lack of menstrual hygiene, and women are often too embarrassed to dry their menstrual cloths in the sun—which means these rags never get disinfected.

In his hunt for volunteers, Muruganantham tried to rope in his sisters. "But after some time, each time I went to ask them something, they would call my mother and say 'ask him to go away.'"

He then tried approaching students at a local medical college. But this was another hurdle—he had never approached an unknown woman and spoken to her. How could he now approach women with this?

There was a big class difference involved. Here was the barely literate son of a handloom weaver facing girls who were studying at a college. It took an enormous leap of imagination for him to try to approach them at all—certainly to talk about menstruation. He even tried asking them for used sanitary napkins—which, to say the least, got him into more trouble in the village. What was a man doing going up to college girls and asking for their used sanitary napkins? But he persisted and eventually gathered enough used napkins to study how absorption of blood happens in various napkins.

Yet he needed more information than the girls would give, so he turned to the only person who could help—himself. He made a contraption that had a football bladder filled with goat's blood and connected it to a sanitary napkin that he wore; wearing that contraption, he cycled to see the absorption of the blood in the pad when it oozed out. He called this apparatus his "uterus"; the goat's blood came from an old childhood friend who was a butcher. The butcher let Muruganantham know each time a goat was about to be slaughtered, and he rushed to collect the blood and get a chemical from another friend at a blood bank to prevent it from clotting. This would go into his "uterus"—and into his sanitary napkin. The one that he would wear when he cycled or walked every day.

This changed his tag—from mad to pervert. Each day Muruganantham went about his work and business wearing his blood squeezer and his sanitary napkins. His wife, Shanthi, who had been patient about his interest, finally left him. This was barely two years after he had first gone to buy a sanitary pad for her.

One of his best anecdotes comes from this period—one Sunday, he laid out many of his bloodied sanitary napkins on a rundown table in the backyard of his cottage. His mother was returning from the village bazaar and saw splattered blood behind the hut.

"She thought, it is a Sunday, so maybe my son has brought home a chicken and is cleaning it up for dinner!"

When she saw what her son was doing, that was the final falling out between mother and son. Like his wife, Muruganantham's mother too left him. "By this time, it had become renowned in the village that there was something wrong with me," he says. "There were many symptoms. I wore a sanitary napkin, I was always doing something with blood and bloody sanitary napkins, and I seemed to be interested in bloody sanitary napkins of other girls but not interested enough in my wife.

"Why else would she have left me? But my mother leaving me was even worse. What would I have done that even my own mother would desert me?"

During this time, Muruganantham would happily put his clothes with blood stains out to dry outside his hut for everyone to see. "That triggered the invisible Facebook and Twitter of the village. You know, every Indian village has invisible Facebook and Twitter. No information or gossip can be hidden—and I had become the biggest topic of gossip!"

He wanted to ask more women for used sanitary pads for research, but it was getting more and more difficult. There was a whole bunch of villagers who came to the conclusion that Muruganantham practiced dark magic. Anything he asked of a woman would put her under a spell.

Then he had to leave the village. His neighbors were threatening to chain him upside down to a tree to try and get the black magic out of him. It had been agreed by the villagers that unless Muruganantham could be cured, some dark spell would fall on the village. For a while, there was serious fear that he might be beaten up.

"This was a really lonely period of my life. From certified depressed and ill, I got termed confirmed psycho and lunatic," says Muruganantham. Then he adds, "The worst thing was that I had to cook for myself." His jokes, often directed toward himself, are perfectly timed, giving the impression that he has long been using them to cover up the old insults.

What Muruganantham was trying to understand was why some sanitary napkins are more successful than others. As far as he could see, most sanitary napkins were made of cotton, but then why were some more absorbent than others? All the laboratory analysis that he had attempted and commissioned on existing pads showed that the core ingredient was cotton. He knocked on the doors of many companies but got no replies until a professor at a local university agreed to help him reach out to some companies. After several phone calls, he finally reached people who asked him what sort of plant he had. "I know they didn't mean a garden and plants in a garden! I of course had no plant, no factory, nothing— and no money to create any sort of factory."

Finally he was able to convince some people to send him samples of standard sanitary napkin material. It turned out that it was cellulose, which was broken down by complex machines and woven into pads with cotton. But he had no machine to do this— and no money to buy a machine. It took Muruganantham nearly five years, but he made his own contraption—a 147-part napkin-making machine that uses a grinder mechanism to break down cellulose and then packs it into rectangular shapes that are then wrapped into cloth and disinfected with an ultraviolet machine. It was a simple, easy-to-learn machine.

"When we look at the problem of rural areas, we say that all these people cannot afford to buy the sanitary napkins that are available in the market. So we are going to make a product, a sanitary napkin, that is cheaper than what the big brands are selling but still does exactly the same job with the same level of cleanliness and hygiene—this is my first target," says Muruganan-tham. "But then comes another equally important question—why are all these people not able to buy this simple product? Because they have no money. Just selling them something cheaper is not enough. What I make also has to create jobs and money in the community where it goes. That's the only way this will be self-sustaining."

When his father, the handloom worker, died, Muruganan-tham's mother worked in the fields as a laborer earning sometimes Rs 20, sometimes Rs 30 a day. He says that made him realize that opening job avenues for women was one way he could contribute. This is why, he says, he did not try to be a manufacturer of low-cost napkins and try to create a "bottom-of-the-pyramid" brand. Instead, he chose to focus on selling the machines themselves. In the meantime, the Indian Institute of Technology Madras entered his machine in a national innovation contest and, out of nearly 1,000 entries, his machine won—and got him an award from the president of India.

This was the moment when he says he decided, resolutely, that he would sell not napkins but machines. In the first two years after the award, he built 250 machines, selling them across India to some of the remotest places. In each place he targeted, he looked at the issues women faced. In Uttar Pradesh, one of his target states since it has some of the worst health statistics for women, Anil Sengar of Srinagar village of Mahoba district told me that in 2013, his four units have sold more than one million napkins under the brand name Subah or "morning." At Rs 18 per napkin, there is no dearth of buyers, said Sengar.

"Women here have to fetch water, walk a lot, do a lot of household work, and using a proper napkin makes a big differ-ence to health and sanitation," says Sengar. "There used to be a lot of hesitation about this subject but increasingly people are willing to talk about it."

He says a lot of myths have been broken about napkins—including that they are not good for a virgin girl's health. Buying from men also used to be a big issue, but that too is increasingly disappearing.

Sengar differs with Muruganantham on one thing. The innovator tends to be a little wary about advertising created by foreign companies to sell sanitary napkins. He feels the focus is too much on style and food and not enough on the critical hygiene issue. "I cannot forget that dirty rag I had seen in my wife's hand," he says.

But Sengar says he doesn't believe fluffy advertisements are a problem. "If something is aspirational, then young girls will buy. Puberty age levels are falling from 13 or 14 years to 9 or 10 years, and the earlier girls know what their health needs are, the better.

"What is wrong in them getting to know this through something that looks like fun and looks nice? At least that way they will be motivated to try it and that's what we want."

Muruganantham's wife is now back with him—as is his mother. And he is back in his village. The villagers have forgiven him and he is well known in the area. Muruganantham says his wife told him that she had no issue with his work when she left him but she could not take the insults of the neighbors.

"This she told me after she returned. Now she is proud of what I do, and we have a daughter. So she knows that it is a matter of pride for our daughter too to have a father who thinks of the problems of women," says Muruganantham.

He and his wife have taken to gifting people who have girl children a set of napkins when the child is born. It is a small message—at least that's how Muruganantham sees it: "Not enough is thought about the future of girls when they are born. My gift is a reminder for the parents to acknowledge and remember their daughter's needs. I don't know whether all of them will remember—but I can try."

Started in 2005, his workshop for the napkins is still small and has only 17 employees who get paid between Rs 15,000 and 30,000 per month. There are no designations. Everyone calls themselves "managers," including Muruganantham. "I didn't have designations for anyone because I didn't really know much about this corporate thing. So if someone asks me what do I do in the company, I say I am a manager," he laughs. The man who used to cycle wearing sanitary napkins now drives a car and earns, "depending on how good the year is," between Rs 750,000 and one million rupees. He has given a TED lecture[2]—as the only man in the world who has worn a sanitary napkin—and has spoken at Harvard. He has presented his business model to a Unilever team in London.

"I cannot believe that a school dropout like me, who taught himself how to speak English and speaks quite bad English, can be invited to speak at Harvard. That is amazing as far as I am concerned. I never believed in my wildest dreams that this would be possible," says Muruganantham. "But then when I went to Harvard I heard lots of famous people dropped out from there too. So I thought, well, thank god I am not the only dropout."

Speaking at TED or at Harvard taught Muruganantham how to explain his vision. He says he was afraid that he would be instantly dismissed as a lightweight for having made a toy. But he learned to tap into the core of his idea. He was not even competing with the multinationals. He did not wish to fight P&G or Unilever. He was showing them the path to all those billions of customers who they were not able to tap.

"The idea is that we are opening doors to worlds where they have not entered. We are doing the hard work of converting the customers and ensuring that they learn what this product is all about and how to use it. Unless we break the taboo, those billions of customers will never get introduced to the product," says Muruganantham. That's why he is spreading his business to other parts of the world. He says he realized that there were poor people in every country and he was selling a necessity, not a luxury.

"The biggest consumer goods companies in the world might try to price something cheaper and sell it to the poor but that is not their core focus—and they don't think of generating employment. As the economic gap between rich and poor keeps growing, there will have to be new ways of thinking about products that can create employment and provide good quality goods," says he. "We are never going to be able to compete with the biggest companies but the customer wants good products, not just brands."

His clients say that, more than money, it is the knowledge he has brought to their communities that is invaluable. Malik Saloni Anand, who set up a unit of six machines in Delhi, says that she paid only around Rs 275,000 for everything including delivery charges, and the machines can make between 200 and 300 sanitary napkins a day. Under the brand name Sakhee or "friend," these are sold in the slums of Mangolpuri in Delhi for about Rs 20 per pad—or about half the price of a branded napkin.

"There are hundreds of women who have learned how to use a pad and whose lives are safer, better because of this machine," Anand told me. "One of the things about doing work with women is that it is not enough to tell them about hygiene issues, one must also provide the solution. Each client can choose whatever brand name they want for the product. Anand said that really helps because it can then be relevant and related to the local context. For instance, in a slum like Mangolpuri, the sense of comradeship between women makes Sakhee a perfect name.

Muruganantham says his desire has always been to ensure that his clients can give a different look, feel and pitch to his core product. "In some places, the target group is school-going girls. In some other places, it is women who work the whole day in the fields and at home—can the pitch be the same? Of course not. As long as the purpose, which is health, comes out clearly and is explained to every customer, it does not matter what it is called."

The project today has a website and the company a name, Jayaashree Industries; on the website are videos of Muruganantham's various talks. Spreading the word has become his passion. He says he travels most of the month telling people about health and his project. In villages and in remote areas, he is sometimes told that his work has made women free to live a little better, has helped girls stay in school, has helped women not be scared of their own bodies. He says that keeps him going. "I am not a woman. But trying to think like one has changed my life, and so I owe a debt to all women."

CHAPTER 9

FACEBOOK FOR THE POOR AND THE VILLAGE CALL CENTER

He used to be a BBC South Asia producer but left to live and work among the tribals of Central India. He has now beaten out Edward Snowden for one of the most prestigious information awards—the Google Digital Activism award of 2014, which is part of the Index on Censorship's Freedom of Expression Award.

Shubhranshu Choudhary has created a network of information (and information gatherers and receivers) among some of the poorest Indians, what he calls a "Facebook for the poor," with the potential to be "Google for the poor as soon as we incorporate 'search.'" Every day between 300 and 500 people listen to prerecorded messages that carry information given by people just like them—all through a mobile phone—on his CGnet Swara network.[1] The system is simple—anyone can give a missed call (dial the number and hang up before a response so that the calling number gets registered but without any charge to the caller) to a number +918050068000 (from outside India) or 08050068000 and immediately the call gets registered at the CGnet Swara call center, which then returns the call via an IVR (interactive voice response) system. The caller can now record their message for a duration of up to three minutes or listen to four previously recorded messages from other callers. CGnet Swara gives voice to the tribal population of Central India by providing them with a voice-based portal where they can report local issues using a landline or mobile phone. The content, once reported, is reviewed by moderators, and the submissions that fit the philosophy and goal of the organization (information for public good) are published for playback on the audio channel. At its heart, CGnet Swara is a voice-based news service.

The idea is to create a citizen-driven, citizen-empowered news and information network that bypasses traditional media entirely and connects a network of consumer-creators. CG stands for Central Gondwana, whose name is derived from an old geological land mass, Gondwana, which consisted of Asia, Africa, and Australia. (In an unrelated coincidence, says Choudhary, the largest tribe of Central India are the Gonds, who are primarily concentrated in Madhya Pradesh, Chhattisgarh and Jharkhand.)

Anywhere between 30 and 50 people call in and record messages, and make it, says Choudhary, the biggest "oral newspaper" for tribals in India. Tribals or people who trace their ancestry to indigenous tribes in India—a bit like the Native Americans—make up a little more than 8 percent of India's 1.2 billion people.

In recent years they have been at war with the Indian state led by Maoist guerillas fighting armed forces of the state including paratroopers. Essentially this is a guerrilla war that is being fought by tribal rebels led by commanders who belong to various Communist and quasi-Communist networks and parties against government paramilitary forces. According to India's Ministry of Home Affairs, nearly 8,500 people were killed in this war between 2003 and 2012.

Choudhary, who grew up in Central India, says he decided to start CGnet Swara in 2003 while researching a book on the Maoist insurgency called *Let's Call Him Vasu: With the Maoists in Chhattisgarh*. He met many young tribals, or "Adivasis," as they are often called, who told him that the violence was largely due to "a communication gap." This is a mild phrase for what is actually a deep and often absolutely bitter disconnect between the world of the Indian tribals and the rest of India, where tribal issues rarely if ever get noticed, unless the news is about tribal guerillas revolting against the state. The tribals of India have hardly any representation in mainstream media.

"The war is a misunderstanding, and behind that misunderstanding is millions of people who just do not have a voice," says Choudhary. "There are people who don't want to be interpreted and re-interpreted by Delhi or Mumbai [Bombay], they want to tell their own stories, on their own terms."

One look at his website, cgnetswara.org, or the institution's Facebook page gives a fascinating sense of how this happens. There are a series of messages that appear one after the other on the page.

One says:

Ramkailash Kol is telling us about a report he had recorded from village Babulaltola in gram panchayat Ghuman, tehsil [a district sub division] Jaba in Rewa district in Madhya Pradesh where 11 widows were not getting their social security pension. He says thanks to calls from friends in CGnet now 6 of them are getting their pension and for the rest the process is on and hopefully they will also get the same soon. I thank all of you who helped.

Another reads:

Jalandhar Singh Porte from village Ghabarra in Surajpur district in Chhattisgarh says they opposed proposed coal mine to Adani company in a public hearing on 20th March and since then local police is harassing them. Their village has got Community Forest rights and some of them had gone to Maharashtra to learn about it but police says we went for Naxal training. Pls call SP [the local superintendent of police] at 9479193900 to stop this harassment.

There is a complaint:

Dilip Behera is visiting Palsani village post Sablahar thana Jhar-ban in Bargarh district of Odisha where villagers tell him that they have a primary school in the village till Class 5. But the school has only one room and all the students study together in that one room and are suffering. They have requested officials many times but there is no response. You are requested to call local officer at 8018882772.

And a solution:

Charan Singh Parte is calling from village Naogawan in Mawai block of Mandla district in Madhya Pradesh. He says I had called on Swara a month back saying there is no electricity in my village and had requested friends in CGnet to call the offi-cials. I am glad to share that today I got a call from officials say-ing electricity for our village has been sanctioned and it will be installed soon. I thank all of you who called the officials.

Each message has a name and a phone number attached to it. This serves several purposes. Local CG Swara volunteers in that area can check the veracity of the message. Also, the organi-zation's 12 full-time employees can call and verify the message, especially if it is a complaint. When the message is in a local tribal dialect, which it often is, a local associate of CGnet Swara in the area where the call came from can transcribe and translate the message and then check its accuracy.

At the moment, the service is free for callers. The network gets two kinds of messages—one from citizen journalists, who have contributed to it in the past, and the other from those who are new to the system. Many citizen journalists who have contributed to CGnet Swara in the past have their messages immediately "filed" and available for hearing; for others, a process of verification, sometimes by a local citizen journalist, is followed. Also, if the complaint is about a government official, the complainant is asked to add the name and phone number of the person against whom the complaint is being made so that CGnet Swara employees can call and check on the situation from the perspective of the official. "We are building a network of reliable informants who can deliver real-time voice-based information," says 44-year-old Choudhary.

One look at the kind of messages CG Swara gets, and anyone who knows India and Indian media knows that these places, these names, almost never figure in the tales this country tells the world about itself, and the ones it repeats to itself. This is a different India speaking to itself and resolving its problems.

Choudhary's work fascinated me because it goes to the heart of the country's democratic debate—what kind of democracy do we really want to be? It goes back to that fundamental question we addressed in the introduction to this book—what kind of democracy does India really need? Measured or experience? Choudhary's bet, like mine, is that India now needs to metamorphose into an experienced democracy. At the heart of his project lies this dream—making democracy an everyday experience of complaint, feedback, redress, and conversation. When I spoke to Choudhary, I realized we both believed that the act of conversation lies at the heart of democracy—and that is what makes his project critical. It allows daily conversation. How did the technology part come to the organization? It came via Bill Thies, a software expert who works at Microsoft's India office in Bangalore and happened to meet Choudhary. Thies, a PhD student from the Massachusetts Institute of Technology (MIT) joined hands with Choudhary to create a platform that could be used to connect disparate voices from the tribal belt. "We were clear on what we wanted—we wanted a simple system that anyone can use, which does not require a lot of education or literacy skills to use. And we wanted a system that could absorb and disseminate information effortlessly and that's what we built," says Choudhary.

What they thought of was this—how can a system be built where tribals could talk about all the things most important to them? Where can they talk to each other about their cow, their chili, their rice? "We began by being Google for the poor—as in people came to us mainly to listen and get information. Now we are transforming also into the Facebook for the poor via voice," says Choudhary, whose project had earlier won a UN Democracy Fund award.

Present radio laws in India do not allow CGnet Swara to be on the medium that is their natural ground. Commercial radio licenses are too expensive and community radio has too short a radius—often barely ten kilometers (about 6.2 miles). "For this 10 km license, you need to take 22 permissions. It is bizarre," says Choudhary. Without a license, there is a citizen band at 26.9 MHz to 27.2 MHz that the law allows people to use, but the receiver is still way too expensive for tribal areas. The cheapest receiver that can catch this band costs about Rs 5,000. Efforts are underway to make different kinds of models to make low-cost servers, including using the Raspberry Pi, the pirate radio transmitter. The dream is to run localized radio stations that would have infinite depth in local information using an army of citizen journalists, most of them trained by Choudhary.

Until then, CGnet Swara is experimenting with various formats—like the song programming they did in 2013 called Sangeet

Swara where anyone could dial in and sing a song and anyone could listen to it. Nearly 100,000 people tuned in.

But for all the attention, Choudhary is often on the radar of government agencies, which have frequently searched his premises, suspecting Maoist misuse of his network. It doesn't help that Lingaram Kodopi, the activist nephew of Soni Sori—who was accused of being a Maoist rebel and tortured in Chhattisgarh (activists have called it a gross violation of human rights)—was trained in citizen journalism by Choudhary. As Sori's case led to global headlines as an example of human rights violations in the fight against Maoists, Kodopi too attracted a lot of scrutiny with his activities, many of which, as a citizen journalist, led back to Choudhary. Kodopi is the first trained tribal journalist from the region.

"Sometimes the government suspects us, sometimes the Maoists do—but neither has ever found anything amiss with us. We genuinely want to be the independent media bridge—otherwise this war will never stop. We will never stop until forced to stop."

Until then, there are some interesting business plans. For instance, Swasthya Swara, a voice-based platform where anyone can discuss herbal medicines or cures and anyone can listen in and access the medication. "We can even stock such pure organic medicines and supply them to anyone who wants them. It will be a completely novel model."

◆　◆　◆

THAT'S THE SORT OF OUT-OF-THE-BOX THINKING THAT BROUGHT ABOUT DesiCrew, which was India's pioneering rural BPO when it started in 2005 and the first one begun from scratch as a start-up by a woman entrepreneur.

Saloni Malhotra, a 23-year-old engineer, heard a lecture in Delhi, given by Professor Ashok Jhunjhunwala of the department of electrical engineering at the Indian Institute of Technology in the southern Indian city of Chennai, that spoke about taking technology to the masses. And so she did. In 2005, she started Desi-Crew in Chennai, incubated under the entrepreneurship program at IIT-Madras, which was run by Jhunjhunwala; she built a company of 600 employees across two Indian states with angel funding from a top-ranking former executive of Infosys, one of India's best-known information technology firms.

DesiCrew started operations as a commercial organization in 2007, offering services in project and content management, digitization, mail-room services, secondary research and transcription, website monitoring, localization of web products and beta testing.

While current venture capital funding does not allow the company to reveal exact numbers, DesiCrew has grown by 50 percent in the past year alone. The idea was to see if the kind of outsourcing work that kick-started an Infosys could be done away from the major cities of India, taking that kind of work to the villages and providing employment there.

"We always said let us take jobs to where people are rather than bring people to jobs. We only wanted to create opportunities for the folks who want a white collar job in their geographies. Why can we not provide the kind of training for basic backend work like data entry, for instance at a small town or village level?" says Malhotra, who opened one center in the village of Kollumagudi, about a six-hour drive from Chennai. The beautiful colonial-style bungalow cost DesiCrew a fraction of what the company would have paid as rent in any city. The company also discovered that while the crop of local employees that they could hire often lacked the external finesse and soft skills that a city hire might have, in the long run the rural employees often turned out to be more stable and loyal.

One of the strategies that the company applied was to first start BPO voice operations in regional languages before diversifying into English. The current CEO, J. K. Manivannan, says his pitch is always that DesiCrew is the place where students from a rural background get a chance to pick up invaluable soft skills.

"There have been many instances where people have spent a couple of years with us and have then moved on to larger BPOs in cities but equally there have been instances when the candidate has tried to make the leap too swiftly and having failed to adjust in a larger pond has come back to us," says Manivannan. He says one of the biggest drives for new employees is to soak up the English language. "In fact, we did not venture into voice mainly because we wanted processes that can be replicated for an international market. For example, a policy issuance for a domestic insurance company can be replicated for an international health-care/insurance company. The focus on English is because in addition to the linguistic skill, in Indian context, more accentuated in the rural areas—knowing English is also a proxy for confidence, self-belief, and worldly exposure. A rural BPO needs to be seen in the context of reinvention of the public skills of the employee." In fact even the term "rural BPO" is hardly ever used these days. To emphasize that the quality provided is on a par with any urban center, the term used is "Impact Sourcing Service Provider."

Veena Shetty is the head of human resources for DesiCrew. She worked at India's biggest bank, the State Bank of India, and at tech and consulting companies like Cisco and Accenture, until choosing to return to a town near Kaup, a village in Karnataka where DesiCrew has another center and where her husband had business.

"It is a delicate balance. On one hand, our aim is to ensure that new employees from a rural background do not get intimidated and absorb at their own pace so that their growth is maximized, but on the other hand, the client is not less demanding of us because we work as a rural BPO," says Shetty. What this means logistically is that DesiCrew had to get government broadband connectivity to Kollumagudi when it started operations there. But it wasn't good enough. DesiCrew now spends Rs 50 lakh ($84,000) in running two separate lines in every center so that there is never a "no connectivity" moment for the client.

When she started building the company, Malhotra, now only 32, traveled across the state of Tamil Nadu (whose capital is Chennai) in buses from village to village trying to grasp what she was getting into. "I ought to have been very scared. I was a young girl, all alone in very remote locations," remembers Malhotra. "But I was not scared. There was a sense of comfort that I felt in those communities which I had never felt in a city. What people there did not have is as much exposure that city folk take for granted.

"We wanted to understand whether given exposure, the model would be competitive—and it is."

Ashwanth Gnanavelu, a founding member of Malhotra's team who has the background of having worked with P&G in Surrey, says the DesiCrew model is to bridge two very disparate worlds. "We have tried understanding that people feel happiest when they get employment at a location that does not uproot them from their social context. This is especially true in India when already such a churn is happening with dealing with modernity in every aspect of life. In such a situation, when a person from a village is able to access the modernity of a BPO job without having to entirely displace themselves from their social context, it is a boon."

In 2012, DesiCrew raised $1.12 million in a second round of funding from responsAbility Ventures I and VenturEast Tenet Fund II.

For Malhotra, Manivannan and their team, what is more important is that in a place like Kaup, where most of their employees had earnings of barely $50 a month, they have been able to double it to more than $100 a month. This means around 80 percent of their employees at this center—and the story is replicated in almost every other center—started saving for the first time after getting a BPO job in their village.

CHAPTER 10

FROM DUNG TO DETERGENT

It happens barely 60 kilometers (37 miles) away from the Indian capital, a medieval practice of discrimination so disgusting that Indian governments and courts have passed law after law trying to ban it. Yet it lives on, barely a two-hour drive from Delhi.

Manual scavenging, one of the worst and most heinous aspects of India's caste system, is practiced, I found out to my horror, barely a few minutes from the new townships coming up in the Ghaziabad area on the outskirts of Delhi. When the outlines of the new towers, full of advertisements of elevators and swimming pools, gymnasiums and crèches (day care centers) end, the road meanders through fields to land in the village of Nekpur in Ghaziabad, Uttar Pradesh.

Manual scavenging is the name given to the task of picking up someone else's human feces with bare hands, placing them on a wicker basket and carrying them to a distant location, often digging a hole, and burying them. This was a task performed by the lowest of lower castes in ancient and medieval India, the untouchables. In the absence of a proper sewage system and compost toilets, this was the Hindu solution. The truly foul thing is that this is a hereditary profession, passed on from generation to generation, keeping millions trapped over centuries. In orthodox communities, there is no escape for the manual scavenger because they would never be allowed into another occupation after performing this task. It's the worst kind of catch-22. The life of the manual scavenger also meant the lowest of low lives—no entry to the home of anyone from any other caste, no touching anyone who is not from the scavenger tribe—virtually no interaction with anyone who is not a scavenger.

As India's cities and towns overflow, and solid waste management systems crumble in most places (as we said in chapter 6, 80 percent of India's sewage goes untreated),[1] manual scavengers have also been forced to enter drains and clean them. Often desperate scavengers get heavily drunk before entering a drain so that they can ignore the stench. Another hidden truth is that one of the biggest employers of manual scavengers in India is the railways—which employ more people than any other single institution in the world, but have failed to make compost toilets mandatory in trains. The continuance of colonial-style open toilets means that the railways continue to informally hire hundreds of manual scavengers every day. Government bodies like the railways can get away with this because most manual scavengers are on informal contracts with no regularized documentation showing the nature of their work.

In her searing book *Unseen: The Truth about India's Manual Scavengers*, Bhasha Singh[2] traveled through 11 states meeting manual scavengers, and she discovered that, in a ghastly practice, the job has no breaks or holidays. The work is done every single day, come rain or sun, with no exceptions for illness or even pregnancy. Singh met people who told her that the community encourages people to start young so that they get accustomed to the job quickly—so there is no minimum age either. In fact, Singh met was a young man of 23 who had been working as a manual scavenger for 15 years.

She also points out that the Indian government sanctioned Rs 100 crores for the rehabilitation of manual scavengers in the budgets of 2011–2012 and 2012–2013 and each time the entire amount went unspent. The ironic reason presented from the government side was that no one who is a manual scavenger was approaching the government to take the monetary support—and by the time the year ended, the government declared each time that there had been no comprehensive study to show how many were actually working as manual scavengers. One of the reasons was perhaps that the government kept insisting before the new 2013 law was passed that there was no or virtually no manual scavenging left in India. To counter this, the not-for-profit Safai Karmachari Andolan presented a document of 15,000 images with names and locations of manual scavengers at work.

That this practice continues in modern India—estimates suggest about three-quarters of a million scavengers in the country at present—is one of the biggest embarrassments for the country.

The law banning manual scavenging, called the Prohibition of Employment as Manual Scavengers and Their Rehabilitation Bill, was passed in 2013, making it strictly illegal to hire manual scavengers, calling for the destruction of all dry toilets and providing for the rehabilitation of people employed as manual scavengers.

On paper, it had been banned since 1993, but not a single person had been charged with the practice in 20 years—hence the need for the new law. According to the 2011 census, there are over 750,000 families that still practice manual scavenging.

But change is coming to the village of Nekpur. A project developed by the Safai Karmachari Andolan and the Delhi-based high-profile economics and commerce college, the Shri Ram College of Commerce, identified 20 women from the village of Nekpur who had been working as manual scavengers. None of them had any access to education, health care or sanitation, nor did they have any real earnings. Project Azmat—an Urdu word for dignity—is the story of how these 20 women became entrepreneurs making detergent that is now sold across the city of Delhi.

The business model has four steps:
♦ Replacing dry latrines with two pit toilets
♦ Providing professional training in the production of the chosen product
♦ Forming a cooperative society
♦ Establishing a successful microenterprise through regular production and sale.

"What we wanted to achieve is not just taking the people away from a terrible way of life but also to give an alternative," Shriyani Sharma, the second-year commerce student who manages the project, told me. "You can give money but just giving money is not enough. If you just give money, it is not a sustainable model. The money will be quickly spent, then what?

"This project answers that 'then what' question. The idea is for us to create a livelihood that keeps them away from scavenging forever."

The women have been taught to make detergent with the help of an industry body, the PHD Rural Development Foundation, and a chemical maker, Chemisynth group. A women's cooperative was created as the foundation that would create a product that could bring a livelihood to these women. A name was created—Neki, the Hindi word for decency, goodness, goodwill, which even has a popular phrase of its own: "'Neki aur puch, puch,'" meaning why ask so many times before doing something good.

Together the women and the students came up with a formula for a detergent. It is now sold in two varieties—Neki Supreme, which sells at the higher end at around Rs 70 per kilogram (2.2 pounds), and Neki Active, which sells at around Rs 50 for one kilogram. At both ends, Neki is as expensive as some of the most popular brands in the market, including Tide and Surf.

Initial testing of the product was done in several venues including the commercial washing areas or *dhobi ghat*s, wholesale and retail outlets, department stores, hostels and residential areas in and around Ghaziabad.

The project in its first year sold about 2,000 kilograms (4,409 pounds) of detergent from 15 selling points in and around Delhi. The profit margin for Neki Active is around Rs 13 per kilogram and for Supreme around Rs 27 per kilogram.

The place where the detergent is made is a clean, single-storied house that has a large lawn, two rooms and a wide verandah. The women work on the concrete lawn or the verandah to mix chemicals for the detergent. They come in around 9:30 every morning and start the day with morning prayers—long kept away from temples of every kind, this is almost a re-induction of these women into normal society.

Rajni Walia, 25, told me that the biggest change that had come into her life in the past year has been that people have started inviting her into their homes in the village. "I thought maybe even after I stop doing the dirty work, no one will want to touch me. But it is not like that. People now know that I work with soap. So everyone thinks I am clean," she said.

The women were earning an average of Rs 300 per month in their earlier occupation—this has gone up to an average of Rs 2,000. "The purchasing power itself has made a world of difference to their confidence," says Sharma. "Now they no longer go to ask a shopkeeper to take pity and give them something. They bring hard cash."

The team is now looking to achieve economies of scale by mechanization and electrification of the production facilities, and to procure long-term contracts with potential demand avenues.

It's hard to believe, but a classic triple-bottom-line project is unfurling at Nekpur village, once perhaps the most ostracized community in India. The project has significant social, economic and environmental impact. New employment opportunity has increased the overall income of the women by 544 percent, thereby empowering them and making them financially self-reliant. This has also inculcated in them the habit of saving, thus ensuring prosperity for future generations. The social impact has been the establishment of a community-owned microenterprise that has instilled in the women a sense of entrepreneurship, enabling them to lead a life of dignity, which has helped to transform the perception of the villagers toward the women. The sanitation conditions of the village have improved drastically, thereby enhancing the quality of life of more than 7,500 inhabitants. The increased income of the women will also lead to greater education opportunities for their children. And finally, the environmental impact is the complete abolition in the village of dry latrines. A breeding place for disease has been replaced with better sanitation systems (by building 128 two-pit toilets) that not only conserve an average of 69,120 liters (18,260 gallons) of water per month, but also supply nutrient-rich manure, boosting the agrarian economy of the area. Coming up next is the installation of solar panels at the production center in order to meet the electricity requirements of the entire detergent-making process in an eco-friendly manner and counter the uncertainties associated with irregular power supply in the area. The regular supply of electricity would massively push up production of detergent from 2,000 to 3,000 kilograms (about 4,400–6,613 pounds) to 54,000 kilograms (about 120,000 pounds). Project Azmat's uniqueness lies in its ability to develop an alternative livelihood for manual scavengers in consultation with the community. In Nekpur, detergent making was chosen as it is relatively easy for the women to grasp and carry forward, considering they have no prior education or vocational training. Furthermore, since detergent is a necessity, it has a relatively inelastic demand in rural and urban areas. There is a dream now to expand the business and take it to neighboring villages where manual scavenging is still prevalent and identify the next community ripe for entrepreneurial transformation.

As Priyanka, one of the women, told me, "Everyone offers me tea now. Earlier no one would let me even touch their utensils."

CONCLUSION: WAS THE MAHATMA A SOCIALIST?

Mahatma Gandhi would have been a good entrepreneur. He was a Gujarati, from the state that has produced India's most successful entrepreneurs, including the Ambanis, and more recently the $8.7 billion Adani Group, whose owner, Gautam Adani, has been a close friend of Narendra Modi, the powerful Gujarat chief minister and now India's prime minister after a historic victory in May 2014—much like the Ambanis are said to have close, and old, ties with the Gandhi family. He took a start-up, the Indian National Congress, to unprecedented and unimaginable heights.

Such ties were the subject of very critical attention in the run-up to the 2014 elections, and rightly so. Indian enterprise has a unique challenge at hand—for years, in the absence of clean and clear government regulation, it has been accustomed to doing business through stealth. Manmohan Singh, prime minister from 2004 to 2014, even described the country's much-treasured economic reforms process as "reforms by stealth." What the prime minister was trying to explain was that sometimes vested political interests could mar the process of economic development by focusing on short-term gain rather than long-term good. So perhaps, the prime minister seemed to suggest in his comment, it is better not to draw too much attention when reform is in progress.

This idea is not new. It was said, albeit in a different way, by the late BJP minister, Pramod Mahajan. During his party's time in power between 1998 and 2004, he praised the rise of the Indian information technology companies as global powerhouses by saying that their growth was helped by the fact that they were based in the southern city of Bangalore (and not in the limelight of Delhi or Bombay) and that when they were growing, not many in Indian politics really understood the business of technology. He laughed and said, only half-jokingly, that had the Indian politicians known about the potential of the industry, its rapid growth would have been impossible.

There is even a phrase for this kind of stealth—"India grows at night." But there is a flip side to this quietude, aptly described by another recent buzzword in Indian enterprise—*jugaad*. At its best, *jugaad* is a spirit of can-do-ness that empowers frugal engineering, a resource-scarce mindset appropriate for a world running out of resources and reeling from the excess of the boom years.

But more often than not, in practice, *jugaad* is an excuse for appalling incompetence, inefficiency and a complete inability to define and live by world-class standards. This mindset of *jugaad* is why India barely makes objects that match the best quality standards in the world. We provide some of the best software engineers to the world, but we have failed at world-class product innovation. The next Apple is not coming from India; neither is the next Microsoft or the next Samsung or Boeing. We did not build Amazon, and now Amazon is challenging even our copycat version, Flipkart, on our turf. Food, water and drugs have unprecedented levels of contamination and imitation in India. We have shown the world that India can buy and successfully run Jaguar-Land Rover, but the same company, Tata Group, has not been able to make a great car in India and failed miserably in their great *jugaad* project, the Tata Nano, the world's cheapest car, which very few people bought. So much for frugal engineering. And in spite of the low-cost Mars mission that has astonished the world, there is little to suggest that India's space prowess will lead to cutting edge low-cost projects elsewhere. This is a country which cannot yet make roads that don't wash away at the first rain in its financial capital, Mumbai.

The "stealth" rule is exactly like *jugaad*. It has a nasty flip side: forced socialism, nationalization and a license-quota regime, all the things that destroy a quest for perfection in India, of getting things just right, of aiming for the highest quality, of pushing the indigenous to the greatest possible levels of global quality.

Each year, when I write *Fortune India*'s annual luxury issue and travel to Europe to interview CEOs of the world's biggest luxury companies, I am newly impressed at their attention to detail. One year, at the Hermès headquarters store on rue du Faubourg Saint-Honoré, I watched a store assistant clean a glass display table top 15 times in 37 minutes, each time with silent, nearly invisible efficiency, as various customers placed their arms or fingers on it. One of the reasons I stopped writing about the business of Indian luxury and fashion is because, after two books, I realized we just did not have the quality focus—though we had history and hand-work tradition in abundance—to create global brands.

Curiously, one of the most Gandhian things I have ever heard from a CEO came from Patrick Thomas, the CEO of Hermès. He told me that Hermès has never used the word "luxury," and does not believe that "just because you can afford it, you should buy ten Hermès handbags." He said, "We believe that our products are meant to last for several generations. That's why we are Hermès. If everyone who could afford it started to buy many handbags, it would not be sustainable. Everything we use—from rare leather to super-skilled labor—is finite. There is only so much of it that is available. That's why we have to produce and sell sustainably. The point is to appreciate the finest quality—but not hoard. Not be greedy."

This is something that Gandhi, who defined the rules for engagement and advocated for sustainable empathy between classes and not for class war per se, would easily understand. He wrote, "The world has enough for everyone's needs, but not everyone's greed" and "God forbid that India should ever take to industrialism after the manner of the West. If [our nation] took to similar economic exploitation, it would strip the world bare like locusts." He would also comprehend easily the focus on restoration and preservation of handwork and handicraft. Gandhi might have been shocked at Hermès's prices—but perhaps not, if he saw the prices through the lens of lifetime purchases and the skill sets they help preserve from generation to generation.

Thomas's thoughts sound odd, even ironic, coming from the CEO of a luxury goods company. But then, Hermès is not just any luxury goods company, and its commitment to maintaining the finest quality of French handcraft has kept that country's best traditions alive and its best craftspeople in business. It is, unfortunately, not something India can boast of—though there are increasing efforts to rescue what is left of our heritage. This failure to create enterprise in heritage also shows in tourism, where India gets barely one-third of the number of tourists that Thailand welcomes.

Lest this point be misunderstood, I want to explain that I feel no personal affinity for luxury brands. Even though I wrote two books on the subject, I have never bought luxury goods and have never used them. I have no intention of demeaning Gandhian austerity—which I personally revere—with a luxury brand comparison. What I do admire is what Europe has been able to do so successfully—take indigenous craftsmanship and preserve it by reinventing it into coveted global brands. With India's near-infinite tradition of handwork—and with the love Gandhi had for handwork—I believe the Mahatma would have been happy to see the work of Indian artisans reach every corner of the globe. And he would not mind if the world paid top dollar for the painstaking handwork expertise as long as the business was honest and eco-logically sustainable. That's why my example is Hermès—and not the bling of many other brands.

While writing this book, I tried to learn whether Gandhi was really as antibusiness as many of our Marxist historians would have us believe. I discovered that I was not the only one who doubted this. The writer Rajni Bakshi, for instance, had been talk-ing about how Gandhi's idea of *sarvodaya* (progress and uplift-ment for all) in essence translates to the modern-day concept of sustainability in business.

In a *Guardian* essay,[1] Bakshi pointed out an unlikely echo of Gandhian thought (at least as radical as Hermès's). She claimed that Hungarian-American investor George Soros embraced Gan-dhian philosophy when he accepted that business is always cre-ated within a social, cultural and political context, not in isolation. Soros is also the founder of the New York–based Institute for New Economic Thinking. Bakshi pointed out several examples of Gan-dhian thought at work in modern economics—from Bhutan's Gross National Happiness to the New Economics Foundation's Happi-ness Index to the Voluntary Simplicity Movement in the United States. Indeed, organic food is a quintessential Gandhian idea—so Gandhi would understand Whole Foods and Trader Joe's, but would also question their prices if they seemed too extreme.

Here's the flip side: Gandhi never would have supported genetic modification of crops as an absolute requirement without question-ing. It would have immediately been unsustainable in his eyes—as it is proving to be in state after state in India. He would have wanted a rigorous examination and a case by case approach.

In the same vein as Bakshi, the Indian columnist and writer Sudheendra Kulkarni has explained in detail in his book *Music of the Spinning Wheel*[2] that Gandhi would have loved and embraced the idea of open-source software and the Internet.

In Gandhi's lifetime, some of India's biggest businesspeople were very close associates, starting with Ghanshyam Das Birla, in whose home Gandhi had been staying when he was assassinated in Delhi in 1948.

So was Gandhi a capitalist? Not quite. Was he, then, a socialist in the sense of seeking to remove private capital and ownership of the means of production? No. In fact, Gandhi wrote categorically,

> I do not want to dispossess those who have got possessions; but I do say that, personally, those of us who want to see light out of darkness have to follow this rule. If somebody else possesses more than I do, let him. But so far as my own life has to be regulated, I do say that I dare not possess anything which I do not want. In India we have got three millions of people having to be satisfied with one meal a day.... You and I have no right to anything that we really have until these three millions are clothed and fed better. You and I...must adjust our wants, and even undergo voluntary starvation in order that they may be nursed, fed and clothed.[3]

From this came his definitive economic theory of trusteeship. Gandhi wrote,

> The rich should ponder well as to what is their duty today. They who employ mercenaries to guard their wealth may find those very guardians turning on them. The moneyed classes have got to learn how to fight either with arms or with the weapon of nonviolence. For those who wish to follow the latter way, the best and most effective mantra is: Enjoy thy wealth by renouncing it. Earn your crores by all means. But understand that your wealth

is not yours; it belongs to the people. Take what you require for your legitimate needs, and use the remainder for society.[4]

There is a temptation to dismiss Gandhi as a Luddite when he talks (elsewhere) about India as a country of idyllic villages or when he opposes mass industrialization, but today more than ever, his warning about extreme industrialization and consumerism creating a labor crisis and destroying the ecosystem seems prescient. Like many of the people featured in this book, Gandhi saw entrepreneurship as the means and not the end. Certainly he did not believe that the ends of entrepreneurship can be evaluated through the accumulation of personal wealth. He wrote:

Supposing I have come by a fair amount of wealth—either by way of legacy, or by means of trade and industry—I must know that all that wealth does not belong to me; what belongs to me is the right to an honourable livelihood, no better than that enjoyed by millions of others. The rest of my wealth belongs to the community and must be used for the welfare of the community. I enunciated this theory when the socialist theory was placed before the country in respect to the possessions held by zamindars [landlords] and ruling chiefs. They would do away with these privileged classes. I want them to outgrow their greed and sense of possession, and to come down in spite of their wealth to the level of those who earn their bread by labour. The labourer has to realize that the wealthy man is less owner of his wealth than the labourer is owner of his own.[5]

In the same essay, Gandhi added,

For the purpose of my argument, I have assumed that private possession itself is not held to be impure. If I own a mining lease and I tumble upon a diamond of rare value, I may suddenly find myself a millionaire without being held guilty of having used impure means. This actually happened when the Cullinan diamond, much more valuable than the Kohinoor, was found. Such instances can be easily multiplied. My argument was surely addressed to such men. I have no hesitation in endorsing the proposition that generally rich men and for that matter most men are not particular as to the way they make money. In the application of the method of non-violence, one must believe in the possibility of every person, however depraved, being reformed under humane and skilled treatment. We must appeal to the good in human beings and expect response. Is it not conducive to the well-being of society that every member uses all his talents, only not for personal aggrandizement but for the good of all? We do not want to produce a dead equality where every person becomes or is rendered incapable of using his ability to the utmost possible extent. Such a society must ultimately perish. I therefore suggest that my advice that moneyed men may earn their crores (honestly only, of course) but so as to dedicate them to the service of all is perfectly sound.[6]

This is the social contract that has been broken in India. And yet, in spite of the corruption and crony capitalism, there appears to have been significant churn in Indian business. Recent research[7] tries to ask the question—if there is so much crony capitalism in India, does that mean that for the last six decades pretty much the same companies have dominated India Inc.?

The research compared the current top 50 companies in India with the top 50 in 1964 and 1990 (the year before liberalization opened up the economy). What did it find? There were only 11 common names if you compare the top 50 companies list between today and 1964—Tata, Birla, Thapar, Goenka, Bennett and Coleman, Singhania, Amalgamations, Bajaj, TVS, Mahindra, and Wadia.

But how about between 1964 and 1990—was there churn in the top 50 list even before India's economic liberalization in 1991? There were only 17 common names—which means that there was considerable churn even before liberalization.

"If 33 of the top 50 conglomerates now weren't part of this league even 20 years ago, it represents a reasonable amount of churn at the top," said *The Hindu* report.

But that's not all. Take the top 10 companies in India today and compare them with the top 10 in 1990. Only three names are common—Tata, Ambani and Birla. Of the remaining seven, only Essar and Mahindra were in the top 50 list in 1990. So five companies in the top 10 list of Indian companies today—Vedanta, Jindal, Adani, Bharti and Infosys—either didn't exist or were insignificant in 1990.

The other thing the report looked at was which companies were contributing to this churn. Were they only tech giants like Infosys or Wipro, companies that were growing because, as Mahajan had said, the political system had not discovered them? Not true, said the study. The churn included companies in infrastructure, like Jaypee, GMR, GVK, Lanco and Torrent (the first three are builders of roads, airports, townships and even Formula One tracks, and the last two are power companies); finance (Sriram, about which you have read earlier, and Kotak); media (the Sun Network of the Maran brothers in Tamil Nadu and Subhash Chandra's Zee TV network); and organized Walmart–style retail, with Kishore Biyani's Big Bazaar and auto ancillaries/forging (Motherson Sumi, Kalyani).

The truth is that it is tough to make a generalization about Indian business today, just as it has always been tough to make generalizations about this vast and diverse country. But one thing is certain—if there is dominance of any community or caste at the top of Indian business today, you can be sure that it is being challenged as never before.

This churn is not merely about who is becoming an entrepreneur, or who is able to become an entrepreneur, but also why people are choosing to become entrepreneurs. What is their purpose?

Many entrepreneurs define their purpose in ways that were improbable if not wholly impossible only a few decades ago. For instance, who would have thought that business, of all things, capitalism, and not just politics, would have such a transformative impact on Dalit life and caste in India; who on earth would have believed that a company can be created for maids? And yet, all of this is true in today's India. Of course entrepreneurship is not a magic wand—it will not solve everything, nor will it solve things instantaneously. But business has—largely—never been thought of as part of the solution in India. It has always been thought of—at least institutionally—as part of the problem. The benevolent state and mercenary private enterprise are enduring myths, neither absolutely true, in India even though our experience in the last decade shows that in most public services—from getting a telephone connection to buying a plane ticket—private enterprise has made things cheaper, better, and more accessible. This, in no way, denies the corruption, the adulteration, and the exploitation that some companies have engaged in—and continue—but where competition has been free and fair, usually the market has veered toward getting customers a better deal. An ever demanding customer base has also pushed companies and entrepreneurs to think hard and innovatively about gaps in the market and services that can be rendered—who would think that an Indian village man would spot a gap in the sanitary napkin market or that mobile phone–based voice networks would emerge as the lifeline in the deepest tribal areas of India where the state has failed to deliver any services for decades, perhaps, in some areas, even centuries? My argument is not, and never will be, that private business can solve all of society's problems—perhaps nowhere, but most certainly not in India. The state has a role to play in ensuring justice, equity and democracy. But for too long the state has interfered and impeded the natural entrepreneurial prowess in India—what business, for instance, does the government in India still have, in running hotels? My plea is that for too long the West has heard what it wants to about India—about the slums and the tech companies but never about the truck-financing socialist entrepreneur, about Maoist rebels but never about the ex-BBC journalist building India's Facebook for the poor in the heart of Maoist-dominated India. To see India as the land of slums or slumdog millionaires is the sort of extreme that makes for great headlines across the world. But there is a vast middle India yearning for change, fighting for change, creating change idea by idea, innovation by innovation. I wrote this book hoping that this middle India, my India, would get some recognition.

The present prime minister of India, Narendra Modi, tells a great story. He was once traveling outside India and was asked, "Do you still have snake charmers in your country?" He laughed and said, "Oh no, that was when we were rich and strong. Now we only have mouse charmers." It is the sort of cliché bursting I have tried, in my own small way, throughout this book.

In a sense, the economic and, often with it, political revolution is coming to India the way Gandhi brought independence, and bringing great social change with it, breaking many prejudices and walls. Not with violence and an uproar, but by slowly chipping away at the problem through careful enterprise. It is going to be a different kind of spring.

ACKNOWLEDGMENTS

This book is about the people who feature in it—and I believe every Indian ought to be thankful to them for their perseverance and fortitude. My dearest friend Ishira Mehta introduced me to many of these people and their stories, and to the Mehta family, including her parents, Preeti and Rupesh Mehta, I am very grateful for all the love that they have showered on me throughout my creative journey.

I would like to thank Emily Carleton, my editor at Palgrave Macmillan Trade, who first embraced this book's attempt to deliver a different narrative of the "India story." The process of renegotiating mainstream narrative is, I believe, the most important role a writer can ever hope to fill, and critical to that process are editors who think similarly.

Also, it has been a pleasure working with Alan Bradshaw who has really delicately guided this book at every step of the way and, excitingly for me, was relentlessly enthusiastic.

Thank you also to Lauren Dwyer-Janiec for all her ideas about where this book could travel and how far it could go.

At *Fortune India*, I owe a great deal to the help and support of D. N. Mukerjea and Brinda Vasudevan for their incessant affection and urging.

If there is one person who is always joyful about everything I do, it is Shweta Punj. I am delighted and thankful for her warmth.

Not one thing in the journey of *Recasting India* would, or could, have happened without Priya Doraswamy, my friend and astute agent. It is an absolute joy knowing and working with her.

NOTES

Unless noted otherwise, direct quotes are from interviews conducted by the author from January 2012 to February 2014. Similarly, unless noted otherwise, statistics cited are from public reports of the companies discussed, or public documents whose references are provided in this Notes section.

INTRODUCTION

1. In October 2010, the Indian capital New Delhi played host to the Commonwealth Games for the first time. A series of embarrassing allegations of corruption and incompetence, including in the purchase of equipment and amenities, marked the run-up to the event. The chairman of the organizing committee, Suresh Kalmadi, was arrested after the event and was in prison for ten months. He is out on bail. The Commonwealth Games scandal caused major public uproar against India's ruling Congress Party and is widely understood to be one of the key causes of ire against the Congress government in Delhi, which was voted out of power in 2014.

2. Subodh Varma, "Income Disparity between Rich and Poor Growing Rapidly," *The Times of India*, July 8, 2013, http://timesofindia.indiatimes.com/india/Income-disparity-between-rich-and-poor-growing-rapidly/articleshow/21410981.cms.

3. Arundhati Roy's observations concerning Antilia, Mukesh Ambani's home in India's financial capital of Bombay, appear in the essay "Capitalism: A Ghost Story," published in *Outlook* magazine in March 2012.

4. Alon Confino, *The Nation as a Local Metaphor: Württemberg, Imperial Germany, and National Memory, 1871–1918* (Chapel Hill: University of North Carolina Press, 1997), 7.

5. The report of the comptroller and auditor general of India, the central audit body, on the auction of telecom spectrum in the 2G band said that irregularities in the distribution of spectrum on a first-come, first-serve basis, rather than through an auction, by the Congress-led United Progressive Alliance government had caused a loss of Rs 1.76 lakh crore to the exchequer. This was widely seen as one of the biggest indications of graft in the government, and then telecom minister, A. Raja, spent 15 months in prison as a result. He is now out on bail.

6. The Indian market research organization divides consumers into various categories depending on the number of members and household earnings.

7. Jean Drèze and Amartya Sen, *An Uncertain Glory: India and Its Contradictions* (London: Allen Lane, 2013).

CHAPTER 1

1. Blair B. Kling, *Partner in Empire: Dwarkanath Tagore and the Age of Enterprise in Eastern India* (Berkeley: University of California Press, 1976), 3.

2. Sati in the 17th and 18th centuries had been celebrated in legends and parables as the ultimate honor for a woman in Hindu orthodoxy. But by the start of the 19th century, as reform swept through Hinduism, more and more people saw it for what it was—a ghoulish, perverse ritual often used by ultraorthodox Brahmins to usurp the property of the dead couple. The abolition of sati is today held as one of the greatest tasks accomplished in the overhaul of Hindu orthodoxy in the 19th century by Rammohun Roy and Dwarkanath Tagore and one of the best things achieved through British rule in India.

3. Makrand Mehta, *Indian Merchants and Entrepreneurs in Historical Perspective* (New Delhi: Academic Foundation, 1991), 81.

4. Claude Markovits, *Merchants, Traders, Entrepreneurs: Indian Business in the Colonial Era* (New York: Palgrave Macmillan, 2008), 19, 20.

5. All interviews, unless explicitly indicated otherwise, have been conducted by the author.

CHAPTER 2

1. Details on J&K Entrepreneurship Development Institute at www.jkedi.org.

2. Mass protests with hundreds of young men pelting stones at security forces in Kashmir began in June 2010 after the killing of three suspected male terrorists who later turned out to be innocent young villagers. The protests mushroomed into weeks of street fights between stone throwers and armed forces. Some of the protests were also politically fueled by the rivals of Chief Minister Omar Abdullah. These have been some of the biggest protests thus far against the large presence of the Indian Army in Kashmir and the army's many alleged atrocities.

3. Jammu and Kashmir Bank annual reports and financials at www.jkbank.net. Angel Broking, Result Update 2QFY14, Jammu and Kashmir Bank at http://bsmedia.business-standard.com/_media/bs/data/market-reports/equity-brokertips/2013-11/13843273580.98208300.pdf.

4. "(J&K) Bank reported healthy operating performance, while asset quality remained largely stable. NII came in line with 23% growth yoy on back of 20% increase in advances yoy. The operating expenses grew by 29% (has been growing 25% and upwards for last few quarters) which was in line with our expectations. Operating profit grew by 17.5% yoy. On the asset quality front, the Gross NPA ratio increased marginally by 2bp qoq to 1.7%, while net NPA ratio increased by 5bp qoq to 0.19%, which appears to a modest increase, given the prevailing weak macro environment and low base of NPLs for bank. PCR for the bank dropped by 195bp qoq, but even then at 92%, it remains one of the highest in the industry. Overall net profit for the bank grew by 12% yoy to Rs 303cr. At the CMP, the stock is trading at 1.0x FY2015E ABV, at a higher end compared to peers, which factors in its better asset quality performance vis-à-vis peers even in a challenging macro environment. Hence, we maintain our Neutral recommendation on the stock." Vaibhav Agrawal, VP-Research-Banking, Angel Broking, on J&K Bank, 2QFY2014 results, November 9, 2013.

5. M. Saleem Pandit, "Four Killed as Zubin Mehta's Concert Begins in Srinagar," *Times of India*, September 7, 2013, http://timesofindia.indiatimes.com/india/Four-killed-as-Zubin-Mehtas-concert-begins-in-Srinagar/articleshow/22392358.cms.

CHAPTER 3

1. For more on the Saradha scam, see Live Mint, http://www.livemint. com/Query/5voTl1zEvA2y3bzBTRRDjO/The-Saradha-scam.html.

2. Baiju Kalesh, "Why Private Equity Firms Follow Shriram Group Company," *Economic Times*, May 23, 2013.

3. Lisa Pallavi Barbora, "What Is a Chit Fund?," Live Mint, April 29, 2013, http://www.livemint.com/Money/TM2QQIfmWRi5mtgcEc6zkL /What-is-a-chit-fund.html.

4. David Roodman, "The IFMR Trust: Not Your Parents' Microfinance," Center for Global Development, April 27, 2009, http: //www.cgdev.org/blog/ifmr-trust-not-your-parents-microfinance.

5. Bindu Ananth, "Sustainability Means Going from Buyer Beware to Seller Be Sure," Live Mint, December 10, 2013, http://www.livemint .com/Money/NNCvhOatfDQeB3d6UjxHDO/Suitability-means -going-from-buyer-beware-to-seller-be-sure.html.

CHAPTER 4

1. Asifa Khan and Zafar Sareshwala, "Debunking the 'Facts' on Narendra Modi and Muslims," *First Post*, November 8, 2013, www .firstpost.com.

2. Sanjay Kumar, "Who Did India's Muslims Vote for in General Election?" BBC.com, May 30, 2014, http://www.bbc.com/news/world -asia-india-27615592.

3. In February 2002, a compartment full of Hindu pilgrims returning from Ayodhya, which has been the site of a Hindu-Muslim dispute over a mosque, was set on fire at a train station in the predominantly Muslim area in Gujarat called Godhra and 58 pilgrims were burned alive. This triggered a nearly three-day-long riot across Gujarat, though most of the fiercest violence occurred in Ahmedabad.

4. Surjit S. Bhalla, "Lessons to Be Learnt from Narendra Modi's Gujarat," *The Financial Express*, October 26, 2013.

CHAPTER 5

1. Michael Sandel, "What Money Can't Buy: The Moral Limits of Markets," https://www.youtube.com/watch?v=GvDpYHyBlgc.

CHAPTER 6

1. "Hiware Bazar: A Water Led Transformation of a Village," IDFC Quarterly Research Note, no. 16, June 2012, http://www.idfc.com /pdf/publications/Hiware-Bazar-rural-water.pdf.

2. "India Wastes 21 Million Tonnes of Wheat Every Year: Report," *The Times of India/Press Trust of India*, January 10, 2013, http://timesofindia.indiatimes.com/india/India-wastes-21-million -tonnes-of-wheat-every-year-Report/articleshow/17969340.cms.

CHAPTER 7

1. Constituent Assembly Debates, November 15, 1948, http://parliament ofindia.nic.in/ls/debates/vol7p6.htm.

2. Ibid.

3. B. R. Ambedkar, *The Problem of the Rupee* (London: P. S. King & Son, 1923).

4. B. R. Ambedkar, *The Evolution of Provincial Finance in British India* (London: P. S. King & Son, 1925), 140.

5. B. R. Ambedkar, *India on the Eve of the Crown Government*, http://drambedkarbooks.wordpress.com/dr-b-r-ambedkar-books/.

6. Ibid.

7. Ibid.

8. Ibid.

9. Ibid.

10. Ibid.

11. Ibid.

12. Surinder S. Jodhka, "Dalits in Business: Self-employed Scheduled Castes in Northwest India," Working Paper Series, Volume 4, Number 2, p. 5, Indian Institute of Dalit Studies, 2010.

13. Ibid., p. 8.

14. Ambedkar, *India on the Eve of Crown Government*.

15. Ibid., p. 14.

16. Ibid.

17. Ibid., p. 18.

18. Ibid., p. 19.

19. Ibid., p. 21.

20. Ibid., p. 22.

21. Ibid, p. 23.

22. Email to author.

23. Thomas Babington Macaulay, *Minute on Education*, February 2, 1835, para. 10, http://www.columbia.edu/itc/mealac/pritchett/00 generallinks/macaulay/txt_minute_education_1835.html.

24. Ibid., para. 12 and 13.

CHAPTER 8

1. Kounteya Sinha, "70% Can't Afford Sanitary Napkins, Reveals Study," *Times of India*, January 23, 2011, http://timesofindia. indiatimes.com/india/70-cant-afford-sanitary-napkins-reveals-study /articleshow/7344998.cms.

2. Arunachalam Muruganantham, "How I Started a Sanitary Napkin Revolution!", TED talk, May 2012, http://www.ted.com/talks /arunachalam_muruganantham_how_i_started_a_sanitary_napkin _revolution.

CHAPTER 9

1. Seema Chowdhry, "CGNet Swara: Spreading a Revolution with Words," Live Mint, November 1, 2013, http://www.livemint.com /Leisure/JLMeY7AwookCpyraa04b0O/CGNet-Swara--Spreading -a-revolution-with-words.html.

CHAPTER 10

1. "Around 80% of Sewage in Indian Cities Flows into Water Systems," *Times of India*, March 5, 2013, http://timesofindia.indiatimes.com /home/environment/pollution/Around-80-of-sewage-in-Indian -cities-flows-into-water-systems/articleshow/18804660.cms.

2. Bhasha Singh, *Unseen: The Truth about India's Manual Scavengers* (New Delhi: Penguin, 2014).

CONCLUSION

1. Oliver Balch, "The Relevance of Gandhi in the Capitalism Debate," *Guardian*, January 28, 2013, http://www.theguardian.com/sustainable -business/blog/relevance-gandhi-capitalism-debate-rajni-bakshi.

2. Sudheendra Kulkarni, *Music of the Spinning Wheel: Mahatma Gandhi's Manifesto for the Internet Age* (New Delhi: Amaryllis, 2012).

3. *Speeches and Writings of Mahatma Gandhi*, 4th Edition (Madras: GA Natesan & Co.), 384–85.

4. M. K. Gandhi, "Theory of Trusteeship," http://www.mkgandhi.org /ebks/trusteeship.pdf.

5. M. K. Gandhi, *Harijan*, 145, accessed from M. K. Gandhi, "Theory of Trusteeship," http://www.mkgandhi.org/ebks/trusteeship.pdf.

6. Ibid., p. 49.

7. Harish Damodaran, "Crony Capitalism? Really?, *The Hindu Business Line*, March 18, 2014, http://www.thehindubusinessline.com /opinion/columns/harish-damodaran/crony-capitalism-really/article 5801300.ece.

INDEX